The Squire of East Hampton

THE LIFE OF

EVAN M. FRANKEL

The Squire of East Hampton

THE LIFE OF
EVAN M. FRANKEL

By Allan Appel

THE JEWISH CENTER OF THE HAMPTONS

East Hampton, New York

Evan Frankel's life has already been so unusual, diverse, and fascinating, and also so meaningful to so many people that I felt with great conviction that a book should be written about him and his achievements.

Shortly after my father, Joseph F. Cullman, Jr., died in 1955, I undertook a similar project. My mother was alive at the time to help, but it still took the remarkable talents of Lael Wertenbaker to produce Mister Junior, *the book about my dad. A year ago, when I decided to initiate a book about Evan Frankel, I thought again of Lael Wertenbaker. I found her name in the New York City telephone book, and called. She was no longer living at that number, but the thoughtful lady who answered was able to get me Lael's new number in New Hampshire. When I got Lael on the phone, she referred me to her stepson in New York, who eventually put me in touch with Allan Appel. Allan has done a fine job on the biography of Evan Frankel, with the great advantage of having Evan's family and many friends to help, and even more importantly, having Evan able to fill in the gaps, as only he could, in his marvelous story.*

I am very pleased to have been the originator of this project, and I am also very happy with the book that has resulted. It gives me great satisfaction that this book has been completed as Evan, still full of vitality, moves into his eighty-eighth year. For all those of us who love and admire Evan, it will be a permanent record of a remarkable man's life, which we hope will last many more years.

— Joseph F. Cullman, 3rd

It is my great privilege to be associated with Joe Cullman in the production of this book, the biography of my dear friend and confidant, Evan Frankel.

In September 1980, my father Samuel, with whom I was very close, died. He had grown up, like Evan, on the Lower East Side, and had the same great zest for living that Evan possesses. When I met Evan in 1982, his love for people and for nature became a great inspiration for me. He has filled a void in my life with a steady affection and wisdom, which to me are invaluable.

A father is irreplaceable, but for me Evan has come close. The record of his personality and accomplishments could fill many books. To have helped make The Squire of East Hampton *possible is, for me, both an honor and an expression of my deep and enduring gratitude.*

— Andrew Sabin

Evan Frankel is larger than life. His tremendous energy, zest, and force are magnetic.

He observes life with great clarity and depth. He has a quick sense of humor and is endlessly amusing and entertaining. He has a passion for beauty that began with art and women and found its ultimate expression in the shaping of his land as a fantasy sculpture garden and wonderland; a passion for tradition that began with devotion to his family and culminated in building the beautiful Gates of the Grove sanctuary at The Jewish Center of the Hamptons.

His contradictions, too, are larger than life. He is gregarious but lives alone; he loves women but has never married. He is fiercely independent but needs his many close friends. He is irreverent but devout.

He has attracted to him people who share and admire his energy and zest. Joseph Cullman, executive, industrialist, philanthropist, and sportsman, for one; Andrew Sabin, naturalist, environmentalist, and gold refiner, for another. Both have been inspired by Evan and have seen to it that this book be written.

Evan has been a counselor, companion, and best friend to me. Whenever I needed advice, criticism, or help, he gave them freely. He inspired me to try to do good while I try to do well. He conspired to have me join The Jewish Center of the Hamptons, and eventually to have me elected its president!

I feel privileged to have Evan in my life, and I am delighted that Evan Frankel's exemplary and very special story is being told. If this book is half as much fun as knowing him, it will be a great success, and then it will help in Evan's ceaseless efforts to support The Jewish Center of the Hamptons!

— Leonard Gordon   President,
The Jewish Center of the Hamptons

AUTHOR'S ACKNOWLEDGEMENTS

Very special thanks are due to Joe and Joan Cullman and to Andrew Sabin, without whom this book would not have been possible. I want to express my gratitude for their assistance and understanding, and their graciousness.

Many other people gave willingly of their time to talk to me about Evan. I want to thank them all for their helpfulness: William Ball, Michael Bassett, Charles Bennett, John Bennett, Raymond Bigar, Paula Blasband, Edward Bleier, Goodwin and Rose-Helen Breinin, Debbie Frankel, Peggy Goldsmith Gillis, Bert and Elena Prohaska Glinn, Leonard and Margot Gordon, Rabbi David Greenberg, Herman Gross, Steven Hahn, Judith Hope, Norman Jaffe, Kari Lyn Jones, Anita Kessel, Dorothy King and the staff of the East Hampton Library, Ann Jones Light, Charlotte and Irving Markowitz, Betty Marmon, Herman Neumann, Charles Osborne, Deborah Perry, Suzanne Pincus, David Plesser, Nancy Plesser, George Polychronopoulos, Jeffrey Potter, Berton Roueché, Harrie Ellen and Tom Schloss, Amy Small, Steven Siegel and the staff of the 92nd Street Y Library, José Tasende, Sylvia Tennenbaum, Emerson Thors, Oscar Weinberger, Bobbi Weinstein, Lael Tucker Wertenbaker, William Wertenbaker, and Enez Whipple.

Ernest Frankel looked over the manuscript carefully. With tact and a deep love for the subject of this biography, he made many helpful suggestions. Finally, and, as always, I want to thank my wife, Suzanne Boorsch, for her patience, astuteness, and good cheer throughout the writing of this book.

— Allan Appel

PROLOGUE

When Evan Frankel returned from the hospital to his East Hampton home in October 1987, he was given four days to live. He was in a delirium for ten days. For two weeks he was unable to speak.

October 1987 - January 1988:

"The *gerator?* The *genator?*" Evan heard the sounds. Then the sounds fell into the shape of a word: Generator. But whatever for? And whose voices were talking about it and floating up to him? Was it his nephew Ernest, who had arrived suddenly from California? And where was Anita now? Had she gone? Was that Joe Cullman's voice, Joan's? And didn't he now hear Harrie Ellen and Tom also, and Margot, and . . . so many people.

The voices floated up to Evan from downstairs. He stirred. He opened his eyes. Thank God, the bed was his own. And here standing around him were his friends, his loyal, beloved friends, and relatives. Here were Emerson and Jane, Andy Sabin, and so many others. And all these people in white. Nurses?

"Evan? Evan?" he heard his name being called, but it was as if from far away. He felt himself dizzy, borne off on a wave, and he closed his eyes.

"You're going to come through this, Evan," the coaxing voices kept up. They would not let him drift off. "Evan, listen:

You have so many people who love you, who need you. Here, look! — A list of all that needs to get done. The temple needs you. East Hampton needs you! Eat some soup!"

He did not feel like eating.

But they were right, all his loyal friends and kin. "The house," he said softly, "feels very warm tonight." But the voice was very weak, and he did not recognize his own words in the infuriating slur that came out of his mouth.

"The *iclitor?* The *inclitor?*"

Now they were asking him to install some other contraption in the house!

"An inclinator, Uncle Manny."

Already he had agreed to a generator, and now they were forcing this inclinator on him, this seat that moved on a track that was to take him up and down his stairs. Like an invalid! And a generator, too! Who the hell needed either of them?

"Lots of people in East Hampton have a generator, Evan, in case the power goes out."

But I'm not lots of people, he thought. I am Evan M. Frankel, and I don't need all these fancy gadgets. I'm going to recover, I am! he told himself, and he would be fine, as always.

But as he sat up in bed, as if to prove it, his arms gave way, and down he fell, exhausted again, weak as a baby.

"Eat some soup, Evan. We have cream of barley today. And cream of mushroom. What would you like? We have cream of everything!"

A spoonful or two. That would be all, but it was good.

Later he heard Ernest's voice again and then those of others — did they include George and Hans from Gordon's? My, *everyone* was here! — discussing him again and that infernal inclinator and the generator. And then, if he could believe his ears, someone had called the Jewish Center and Betty Marmon told them not to worry, she was in charge of the chairs, and there would definitely, absolutely, be enough chairs for all the guests coming to his funeral.

And who was that they were suggesting carry his coffin? Not that sonuvabitch! Off the list with him!

Well, that was just about enough of coffins, generators, and inclinators. Evan sat up in bed. Now he stood and made his way to the top of the stairs. This time he determined to bellow. The pronouncement came out far softer than the roar people had been used to these past eighty-five years, but they were the first strong words he'd uttered in weeks: "The Lord of the Manor," Evan M. Frankel decreed, "will make his own decisions. He is not dead yet!"

Indeed he was not, but it had been a very close call.

Evan had been stricken on October 4, 1987, ironically, on the holiest day of the Jewish year, Yom Kippur. Tradition has it that on the Day of Atonement, "Who shall live and who shall die" is determined, and the Book of Life is sealed.

At first it seemed that Evan had been penciled in on the wrong side of the ledger. He'd been presiding, along with Rabbbi David Greenberg of the Jewish Center, for about four hours on the *bemah*, the dais, beneath the large High Holiday tent erected beside the new sanctuary. Dedicated only a year before, Gates of the Grove was the culmination of a decade of Evan's impassioned work as the Center's patriarch and leader. This Yom Kippur was dank, rainy, and cold, and, as prayers drew to an end, Evan's hands grew icy. What's more, he'd been in a draft all day, and he now as always had to shake hands with over a thousand worshippers. It was a record crowd, and only one of the many signs of the great vitality of the Jewish Center Evan had helped to found and make flourish on the South Fork, where none had existed before.

After all the efforts of this long cold day, demanding for even a young man, let alone for an unusually vigorous eighty-five year old, Evan felt weak. He was taken home by a friend. The following day, he fell. He was found by his house man. Betty Marmon came and drove him to the hospital. Now illness caught up to him with a vengeance: fevers and delirium, then pneumonia, then malnutrition all had Evan down for the final count. His niece Anita Kessel rushed up from Florida. As Evan's condition continued to worsen, his nephew Ernest Frankel, who had been with him for the High Holidays, flew back from California.

When Evan finally came home from the hospital, he was still gravely weakened from the effects of the pneumonia. The doctors in the hospital and another who visited concurred: there was little hope. Other relatives arrived, and a score of devoted friends from a long lifetime hurried to Evan's side. Everyone wanted to help, but the situation seemed no longer in human hands. There were hushed medical conversations. Preliminary plans for a funeral were carefully prepared. Evan's friend Ed Bleier wrote an obituary.

But Evan fought back. His goddaughter Harrie Ellen Schloss and her husband Tom fed Evan water by the spoonful during the night. They spelled Ernest, who had taken charge and was working day and night to have Evan do what he needed to survive — eat, drink, move. When, still depressed by his slurring speech, Evan's spirits flagged, Ernest told him, "I won't let you die. God won't have you . . . or the devil either. You're too damned ornery to die!"

There was a flicker of a smile in Evan's eyes, the hint of laughter, and Ernest now knew that Evan could make it if he only ate and drank. Ernest knew how much Evan respected Joe Cullman. He called, and Joe came the next day. Without a long lecture and without raising his voice, Joe read Evan the riot act: he had to eat, drink, and walk in order to get well and live. From that day on, Evan's nephew Ernest, a former Marine Corps officer in three wars, who had held many a dying man in his arms, was able to orchestrate the miracle of Evan's recovery.

When, by the end of December, Evan was stronger, Ernest asked Evan's close friend and the new president of the Jewish Center, Leonard Gordon, what he should do with the obituary and the funeral plans that had been prepared. Leonard said, "Let's show them to Evan. Go over them with him. I bet he'll love it!"

Leonard Gordon picked up what happened: "We did show Evan the plans, and, sure enough, I was right! He began making corrections and additions, going over his obit, reviewing his funeral arrangements. Evan said, 'What do you think about being cremated? For a lot of Jews, being cremated is a *shanda*, a shame. So what do you think?'

"I told him it was his choice, and then he said, 'Cremation, yes. But what shall we do with the ashes?' I reminded him that he had organized a funeral service at Hook Pond in East Hampton where we had scattered the ashes of his friend, my wife Margot's father. Evan thought for a minute and then said, 'Sounds right to me, but what pond should we use?' So I suggested a pond. 'Terrific,' he said. Finally, however, he said, 'On second thought, I don't want a pond. I want the ocean. I love the ocean.' So I said to Evan, 'Okay, but the only problem is if you get a sea breeze, it can blow back all your ashes over us.' Evan said, 'Well, that's true, but you'll be able to dust it off.' I told Evan not to worry about his dust on us, and he said, 'Wait for a land breeze, but please use the ocean.' That was the kind of conversation we were having. Only with Evan!"

Later, Rabbi David Greenberg of the Jewish Center spoke to Evan. He recalled, "Evan was not Lear on the heath crying, 'Why me? Why me? Why was the wind invented except to torture me?' On the contrary," Greenberg said, "Evan was as down to earth as ever a human being lying on what might be his deathbed could be. 'Look,' he said, 'it happens.'"

Fortunately, it did not.

By the new year, when Evan was clearly on the road to recovery, the physician treating him said, "After seeing what Evan Frankel did, I won't ever count anybody out again."

Evan's eighty-sixth birthday was on January 12, 1988, and his closest friends threw a party for him to celebrate what they called the "miracle birthday." But there was really nothing new about all this. Evan had been doing it all his days, overcoming obstacles, surpassing expectations, and living a life like an unfolding American dream.

I

Evan Frankel was born on January 12, 1902, the youngest son in a large orthodox Jewish family of six boys and four girls, in the tiny agricultural hamlet of Bukochevich in the Carpathian Mountains, not far from Cracow, Poland.

At the time, this area of Poland, known as Galicia, was part of the Austro-Hungarian Empire, and on the walls of even the humblest homes — like that of the Frankels — hung a portrait of Emperor Franz Joseph. Although he was a beloved and enlightened monarch who abolished some centuries-old anti-Jewish restrictions, the Emperor's policies were too little and too late to stem the massive emigration of Galician and other East European Jews to America. It was to be a Jewish exodus, in the opinion of some, quite as significant as the one from Egypt, in that it changed the face of Europe, of America, and specifically of New York City, forever.

Although not impoverished, the Frankels lived a life of few comforts in Europe. Their house in Bukochevich had a dirt floor. For warmth during the cold Polish winters, the children slept on beds stacked one on top of the other like so many shelves, on either side of the fireplace. A creek behind the house provided the family with water.

Evan's mother Nache — to become Nettie in America — came from the Kleinfeld family, which for at least two generations had operated a depot in Bukochevich. This was a kind of inn, with stables, for the traders in grain who would come up from Hungary, and for peasants journeying to the markets in

Cracow fifty miles north. Here, at the Kleinfelds' depot, they would stop, relax, and refresh themselves and their horses. The inn, owned by Evan's maternal grandfather, made that side of the family comparatively affluent.

Evan's father, Abish Frankel, came from a family far more scholarly. Indeed his father was slated to become a rabbi, and he devoted himself to studying, which, according to law and custom, was the highest occupation — the occupation of the mind — to which a young Jewish man might aspire. An itinerant *shadchan*, a marriage broker, spotted this tall, bright, eighteen-year-old fellow and proposed a match with Nettie, who was even younger. Since the prestige of Nettie's commercial family would be enhanced by such a scholarly alliance, a deal was struck, and Nettie and Abish were married.

Such was love in Bukochevich. As Evan himself succinctly put it of his mother's family, "They had money, and now what they needed — and purchased — was wisdom!"

It was a reasonably good marriage. Early photographs of Evan's mother show a woman with a beautiful light-complexioned face framed by thick dark hair pulled up into a bun that settled over her head like a crown. There was a remarkably strong bearing about her, a presence and an independence that she would bequeath to her children, whom she proceeded to produce without delay. First born was Aaron in 1881, followed by Annie three years later, then Yetta, and Mayer in 1890. Four more children followed in the next decade, one girl, Frieda, and three boys, Phil, Irving, and David, who was born in 1898. The two babies of the family were born into the twentieth century, Evan in 1902, and his little sister Claire, in November 1904. There had been, in addition, two other births, but both children died in infancy, of the cholera epidemic that periodically swept through the Galician countryside.

The lingua franca was, of course, Yiddish, and all the children had Yiddish names. Evan's was Meshulam, whose precise correlative in English is Makepeace. Years later in New York, as the Americanization of Evan got under way, he acquainted himself with the English classics and came across the novel *Vanity Fair* by William Makepeace Thackeray. For the briefest moment Evan considered changing his name to Makepeace Frankel. But would *Vanity Fair*'s author, he wondered, have called himself William Meshulam Thackeray?

After his marriage, Abish Frankel went into the egg business in Bukochevich. In the summer, when the chickens were laying, he maintained a large square pit that he filled with lime and then loaded with eggs. The lime served as a preservative, so that in the winter he could still extract eggs and sell them to support his growing family.

The business was hard, the living hand-to-mouth. The "lime pit" and other similar stories of Europe entered the Frankel family's collective memory, told, embroidered, and re-told in America, especially by Evan's oldest sister Annie. It was her reminder to the family that as tough as conditions were on the Lower East Side — to which destination the family was headed — in America at least there were no lime pits, but rather, great hope and limitless opportunities. The Frankel family, and Evan in particular, would make the most of them.

Following a pattern already well-established by the turn of the century, the Frankel family sent its oldest son to America first. Aaron, who was always called by his middle name, Louis, came by himself at age thirteen, in 1894. His goal was to get a foothold in New York, to save money — perhaps $1 per week out of a meager $6 salary — in order to send, the next year, for the next oldest sibling.

Aaron was not utterly alone when he arrived in New York,

however, as a group of Kleinfeld uncles and cousins had immigrated several years before, in all likelihood with some capital.

Aaron, having saved some money, sent back to Bukochevich, and the next installment of Frankels arrived in America — brother Mayer, sisters Annie, Frieda, and Yetta, and Phil. Phil, however, was diagnosed as having glaucoma and failed the eye examination at Ellis Island. On his own, he was sent back to Bukochevich.

For a brief time, Annie lived with increasingly prosperous Uncle Isaac Kleinfeld on the Upper East Side. There she developed a closeness to that side of the family that would endure a lifetime. She worked in a cigar factory and helped find jobs for her sisters. Soon everybody was working, and Aaron had even been able to start in the dry goods business. When Aaron and Annie next wrote home, they suggested the time had arrived to reunite the family.

Although all of his older children were now in New York and he and Nettie missed them terribly, the decision to leave Bukochevich was not an easy one for Abish Frankel. As a man deeply devoted to fulfilling the six hundred thirteen commandments of the Jewish faith, he surely read with trepidation the sensational newspaper and pamphlet reportage about the breakdown of Jewish life in idolatrous America. There were many accusations that American rabbis and *shochets,* the ritual slaughterers, were charlatans. How, Evan's father wondered, could he be sure the meat he bought would truly be kosher? How could he lead a Jewish life and bring his children up as Jews in such a foreign place? And yet, should not the family be together?

As it turned out, the conscription officers of Emperor Franz Joseph's army, knocking at the door of the Frankel residence, helped Abish make the decision. Recalling the family story, Evan said, "As an ardent Jewish scholar, Father had misgivings about leaving Europe and its Hebrew academies for an America he didn't know or trust, but the primary reason he decided to leave was the draft. Even though he had ten children, he was still subject to military service. In the Emperor's army, it would be impossible to eat kosher food. And *that*, and not some bullet, would surely have killed him."

So with baby Claire in Nettie's arms, and two-and-a-half-year-old Evan toddling along nearby, perhaps holding Dave's and Irving's hands and straining to hear every word of thirteen-year-old Phil, the Frankels left Bukochevich. They traveled northwest by train to Bremerhaven, Germany, where they booked passage to America.

The immigrants' journey across the North Atlantic was not only an ocean passage, but a kind of rite of passage as well. Many of those who remained behind — Evan's father was the youngest in his family and left two sisters in Europe — were never seen again by the family in America. But for the young, like Evan, not weighed down by what was behind, America beckoned and made her golden promises to those who could distinguish themselves from the rest of the immigrant crowd.

Evan lost no time in doing precisely this. One of his earliest memories is of this voyage: "On the boat coming over I became the pet of the crew. They always brought me up from steerage to the deck. I was a round-faced kid with big curls, and I guess I amused them. In return I got all sorts of goodies, one of which was a 'marantz,' an orange. In our town, a cold place, an orange was a rare treat, so imagine how much rarer on a ship on the Atlantic in the dead of winter! Yet the crew fed me one each day until we arrived in New York."

Although the Frankel family, like nearly everyone else aboard, traveled in steerage, Evan, through his charm, had managed to transform it, in this fashion, into something of first class. The "marantz" story, too, became part of the fabric of Frankel family legend. More importantly, it entered Evan's early consciousness of himself, a sign of how he might play a large role in life as he already had on the immigrant ship.

The Frankels arrived at Ellis Island in the winter of 1905. This time, Phil passed the eye examination, and the family was registered, processed, and then ferried to Manhattan. They debarked at Desbrosses Street, where they were reunited with Aaron, Mayer, Annie, Frieda, and Yetta. A horse-drawn trolley took the family from the pier to a tenement on the corner of Pitt and Hester Streets. Aaron had by now married, but the rest of the family lived here together, in a fourth-floor apartment. It was to be the first of many addresses the Frankels would have on the Lower East Side.

This first home in America had a living room at one end, the kitchen at the other, and, in between, several small bedrooms. The toilet — not much more than a country shed — was in the yard four flights below.

By contrast, the Kleinfeld uncles were all well-established when Abish and Nettie arrived with Evan and the last batch of little Frankels. Uncle Isaac Kleinfeld had already built up a business, the charmingly named Okay Ice Cream Company, which delivered ice cream to the ghetto. Well-dressed, "uptown" Uncle Isaac was particularly fond of his sister, Evan's mother. His frequent visits to the Frankel home impressed his nephew at a very early age — a living example of success and prosperity, American style. Years later, when young, dashing

Uncle Evan, in raccoon coat, driving a long shiny Packard, swept into the lives of his brothers' and sisters' children to dispense presents with style and grace, he was, in all likelihood, playing the same high-flying role: stirring, as Uncle Isaac Kleinfeld had, the dreams and ambitions of his nieces and nephews.

The extreme congestion in which Abish Frankel and his family now lived was, however, the norm for the Lower East Side at the time. Official 1905 population tallies for what was then known as the Jewish Tenth Ward recorded a density of 1,500 people per acre. Hester Street was one of the main market streets, always thronged, and at Hester and Ludlow, just a few blocks away from the Frankels' first home, was an intersection dubbed "Chazzer-Mark," in Yiddish, or "Pig Market." Small garment contractors would go there to select a handful of men and women who would work in the boss's crowded home, sewing for long hours and little pay. It was the origin of the sweatshop. Yetta and Frieda, before they got jobs in the developing garment factories, might well have gone down the block to Hester and Ludlow for the early morning shape-up.

Overcrowding, unregulated labor, and inadequate sanitary conditions were the bad side of ghetto life, but there was also the great vitality and promise that even the youngest Frankel children sensed in the Yiddish and English cries of the peddlers that filled the streets. Moreover, one was rarely alone. If the family members worked and pulled together, each contributing to the whole, all might advance. The two essential realities of the Lower East Side were work and hope, and if you got into trouble, you could be helped by a *landsmanschaft*, an association devoted to helping newly arrived immigrants from the same town in the old country.

In 1902, just a few years before Evan's arrival on the

Lower East Side, an important book, *The Spirit of the Ghetto*, was published describing life there. Its author was Hutchins Hapgood, a descendant of seventeenth-century New Englanders whose Puritan relatives founded East Hampton, where Evan would himself settle in another half century. Hapgood wrote, "Individuals and groups who represent what might be called the underdog, when they are endowed with energy and life, exert pressure toward modification of cast-iron habits, and lay rich deposits of cultural enhancement. . . . " This was to be an apt and prophetic description of the Frankels, Kleinfelds, and the more than ten million Europeans who came to our shores between approximately 1900 and 1910, and who would proceed to transform the next seventy-five years into the American Century.

The Frankels stayed at Pitt and Hester for less than a year. The next address was only two blocks away, on Sheriff Street, running parallel to the nearby East River. In general, families didn't stay in a place for more than a year or two. And newly married couples — Aaron had married in 1904, Annie in 1906, and Yetta in 1908 — were among the most peripatetic. As a little more money came in — earned by the unmarried children old enough to work — that money bought a little more light and a little more space. It also brought more proximity to grass and water. Evan's attraction to both was to be an important theme in his life.

The center of Frankel family life outside the home was the synagogue on Sheriff Street, Anshe Sfarad of Bukochevich, loosely translated as Bukochevich's Western Sons. Each family from Bukochevich and environs who could afford it contributed monthly to the support of this local countrymen's synagogue. Who is to say that Evan, although very young, did not absorb on Sheriff Street, if only by osmosis, lessons in temple-building he would apply seventy-five years later among his East Hampton countrymen!

Evan's father was a highly respected member of Anshe Sfarad. His learning was such that he was consulted as an authority on fine points of worship and liturgy. Although he was not a rabbi himself, his erudition was at the very center of his life. He even applied it at his trade, which, adapted to America, was that of an egg candler. Culling eggs by holding them up to a light source — often a candle — Abish detected any drops of blood, which would render the egg ritually unfit to be sold to Jews.

In the Frankel home books were everywhere. There were prayer books, the Talmud, the *Shulchan Aruch,* and the great twelfth-century code of the Spanish rabbi Moses Maimonides, *Guide for the Perplexed.* But Abish seems rarely to have been perplexed; he never relinquished an iota of his orthodoxy in America; and when he wasn't working, he was, as was customary, always studying, intoning the ancient text with the joy of utter concentration as he sat beside an open window.

Such a strong figure cannot but have had a powerful effect on his children. Although all the Frankel progeny would remain strongly identified as Jews, only Annie, of all her siblings, would remain strictly Orthodox. Time and again she was recognized as "Jewish Mother of the Year." However, Evan, the youngest of the boys, took away perhaps an entirely different lesson, one Abish Frankel would have approved: a deep love for reading and language, and, above all, an appreciation for the power and influence of words.

Before he went to public school, Evan, at the age of five, went to a Hebrew school, but the lessons were interrupted or cut short by continuing family moves. After Sheriff Street, the Frankels moved to Fourth and Avenue D, and then to Sixth Street between C and D. They were at last away from the heart of the ghetto.

They were still poor, but they were economically on an upward march. Evan saw Central Park's green for the first time on a trip to visit Uncle Isaac on 97th Street. "What a spectacular treat that was," Evan told everybody, and he kept looking forward to more such trips to the park, with its air, water, light, and green grass.

More often than not, however, Uncle Isaac came downtown to visit, because all the Frankels and the Kleinfelds lived perhaps within a single thronged mile of each other, and Isaac might efficiently see them all. To Evan and the other young children, Uncle Isaac was an increasingly important presence, the "patron" who had truly made it in America. He was living in one of the most fashionable Madison Avenue neighborhoods, had become a large property owner in Queens, and even had a son in medical school. He was always impressively dressed, and he generated, Evan recalled, tremendous excitement during his Rockefeller-style visits: "He would come down to visit my mother, and each of us would get a dime from him. How we would look forward to that! Then we would run around the corner to a bakery that specialized in Charlotte Russe and buy one. That was the height of luxury! Or, for that same dime, we might go to the delicatessen and get four thin slices of bread —not the tough hard rye bread we usually ate — but four beautifully thin slices of white sandwich bread, and on top of it a waxed cone of mustard! That was heaven."

Such heavenly visitations notwithstanding, the daily reality of the ghetto — for children, too — was work and then more work. Aaron developed his business into a dry goods store on the corner of Second Avenue and St. Mark's Place, and Mayer was his assistant. The younger children, Irving, Phil, and Dave, did what work they could find. Sometimes Evan tagged along, especially with Dave and Phil, with whom he was growing close. More often than not, however, the place of the youngest children, six-year-old Evan and four-year-old Claire, was at their mother's side. Perhaps Nettie kept them near because she had become sick and sensed what the future held; for in 1908 she had only two more years to live.

II

In these years, each new bridge, tunnel, or transportation link was altering the pattern of settlement in New York. When the Brooklyn Bridge was completed in 1883, it had enabled an earlier generation of German and Russian immigrants to put down roots in Brownsville. In 1904 a new subway linked City Hall to 145th Street; and in 1905, approximately when the Frankels arrived in New York, the Interborough Rapid Transit system established a line connecting Brooklyn and New York. As a result, the shift in Jewish settlement was fast and dramatic, with a full forty percent moving to Brooklyn between 1900 and 1920.

By 1908, the Frankels were doing well enough to move to Brooklyn, specifically to New Lots. This, unlike their previous moves, was no mere address change. It was a dramatic change in environment that profoundly affected the whole family, and Evan in particular. In New Lots the depths of the ghetto were left far behind. Here was easy access to parks and open spaces. Indeed, New Lots was country — new lots with newly-built houses on them, laid out on flat land at the edge of a marsh. Young Evan, awakening then into full boyhood, delighted in the trees, the grass, and the croaking of frogs at the water's edge.

"New Lots then," Evan said, "is what East Hampton was when I came out here." In a sense, therefore, Evan's falling in love with East Hampton, which occurred forty years after the move to Brooklyn, may have been not only the discovery of a place beautiful and new, but also perhaps a *déjà vu*, the serendipitous *re*-discovery of his New Lots boyhood home.

In New Lots the large Frankel clan finally had a row house all its own with three bedrooms downstairs and four up. Evan's world was expanding as he entered public school. But there was a negative side to New Lots as well. The area had attracted other ethnic groups. There were clashes, not ugly and malevolent gang wars, but clashes over territory. New Lots may have been beautiful, but it was no longer the Lower East Side, and a young boy was continually aware of turf. It was not only an awakening but also a sobering and maturing seventh year for Evan.

It was made more sobering by the onset of his mother's cancer. The family pulled together. The sacrosanct Friday night Sabbath meal became more important than ever, more memorable. From the last year of his mother's life, Evan remembers the candlelighting ceremony, his mother singing the blessing, her hands extended over the flames. Then it was off to *shul*, the up-and-coming family moving proudly and smartly down the street. They were led by Evan's father in his Prince Albert coat (dubbed the Prince Isaac by the new Americans). The tails and silk top hat were donned every Friday night to greet the Sabbath Queen. At home, after services, Nettie served up the elaborate meal, always including fish, chicken soup with matzo balls, and boiled chicken. It no doubt took a great deal of faith, even for Evan's father, to know what he did of his wife's illness, but still not question God's ways.

Nettie finally was hospitalized at Mt. Sinai in Manhattan, but there was no hope of arresting the disease. Evan's first visit to his mother in the hospital was close to traumatic. She was in a large open ward, he recalled, and it was, in his carefully

chosen word, grievous to see her there. By his next visit, however, with the end apparently near, his mother had been
moved to a private room overlooking the beautiful rocky
meadow across Fifth Avenue in Central Park.

It provided some small comfort to a boy as sensitive as
Evan, and so close to his mother, to know that she died in
dignity and in view of Nature. And yet, he was also full of
dismay and rage that she had left him. The year was 1910, and
Evan was eight years old.

After Nettie's death, the family sat the required *shiva*, the
mourning period, and then decided they could not remain in
the New Lots house, the scene of their recent unhappiness.
They moved back to Manhattan, to an apartment on Ninth
Street and Avenue C, an area still well out of the center of the
ghetto and in surroundings that Claire, Evan, Dave, and the
other children might not associate with their mother. At least
some open space, Tompkins Square Park, was nearby, as well
as a public library and a boys club.

Evan was now without a mother, but he was not without
mothering. By the time of Nettie's death, Annie and Yetta had
married and were soon the mothers of children not too much
smaller than their baby brother. As space and circumstances
permitted, Evan's sisters proceeded to take him into their new
homes and to provide him with the care that he could no
longer get under his widowed father's roof. But, of course, it
was not the same.

He went to Public School 188 on Houston Street now, but
after school he commuted to the home of one of his sisters.
Annie, Yetta, and Frieda had all prospered, and moved with
their families to the new community of Borough Park. If, un-
derstandably, Evan had been spoiled and doted over as the

youngest boy in the family, that chapter of his life was now closed forever.

He began to learn quick lessons in independence. Indeed, with the birth of Annie's first son, nine-year-old Evan was already an uncle several times over. Evan's oldest sister, a warm, strong, dominating personality, immediately became a kind of mother substitute for him. However, the crunch of her growing family — five more boys would be born — made it advisable for Evan to stay with Yetta part of the time. Then, as Yetta's family grew, Evan moved to Frieda's for a few months, and so on. If he and Claire tired of sisters and wanted to spend time with a brother, Aaron and his wife were also always happy to take them in. Thus passed years eight to twelve for Evan, in a kind of permanent shuttle from one brother's or sister's home to another.

It was perhaps at this early stage, when he might have felt it was required of him, that Evan honed his innate charm and realized fully that he could amuse, entertain, and really enter talking. For although he was always embraced and welcomed by his extended family, was he not also always a kind of permanent "Beloved Guest?" No matter how adoring and helpful his siblings, Evan surely felt at times the extra wheel, denied, left out, and forced to grow up very, very fast.

It became evident to him that he must now use his skills to distinguish himself in school, to make sure he would receive there the attention that had been so suddenly wrenched from him at home.

Evan read omnivorously and, combining that with a natural gift for language, he excelled, earning at school the nickname "Kid Dictionary." "I just loved words," he recalled, "especially poetry." While Yiddish was spoken more by the older children in the Frankel home, particularly to elders, there was increasing use of English, too. Irving was an avid reader, and brothers Phil and Mayer, Evan remembered, also spoke good English, had good diction, and were great examples for Evan to follow. But "Kid Dictionary" was a real phenomenon: "From as far back as I can remember," he said, "the other kids — and the teachers — used to stand me up and fire words at me; I knew them all."

Today it is hard for us to grasp fully the great importance that shedding of accent and mastery of spoken English had for the immigrant generation of our grandparents. Contentious logomachists, they used to discuss vehemently on the street corner the correct pronunciation of the phrase "bread and butter." And if you could pronounce one hundred words in English, God help the fellow who persisted in calling you a new arrival, a "greenhorn."

In such a world, what a young ghetto Pericles Evan must have been! Early on he was marked by family and friends to pursue that preeminently verbal profession, the law. Evan: "For kids trying to raise themselves up out of the ghetto, studying to be a lawyer was the place to start. Particularly since my father was a scholar of the law, the Jewish Law, it was fitting. I know my father and the whole family wanted me to become a lawyer. It was natural. I spoke at school assemblies from the very beginning. Henry Wadsworth Longfellow's *The Song of Hiawatha* was the first of many poems I memorized and delivered. And whenever I was called upon to read, I did it with great fervor."

Evan's closest friend from this period was Edward Weinfeld, who lived around the corner on Eighth Street, not far from Aaron's store. Evan may well have confided to Edward,

35

who would go on to become a New York State Supreme Court judge, that it was not the law, but language, that Evan really loved. But he was only ten and perhaps didn't yet know that himself, or, if he did, did not want to disappoint his father. What Evan did know was that even though he was poor, if he worked hard, he was definitely going places.

That summer of 1911, the year New York City was rocked by the Triangle Shirtwaist Company fire, Evan was peddling Wrigley's chewing gum. Although in previous years he'd worked running errands and helping his brothers at their employment, this was his first full-time summer work and certainly his first sales job. Evan's "territory" was the Williamsburg Bridge, which he traversed under the hot sun of the long summer days, hawking his Spearmint and Juicy Fruit until his leather carrying tray was empty. If Evan has told and retold this story to relatives, to young friends starting out in business, to temple members during a Friday service, and to more than one interviewer over the years, it is not merely to describe the long arc of achievement his life has traced. The young chewing-gum salesman quite clearly made some important self-discoveries on the Williamsburg Bridge. He discovered he was superb at sales, that he enjoyed working on his own and meeting the whole human panorama that the great bridge paraded before him, and that he loved moving about beneath a vault of sky, preferably near water. These insights would guide Evan throughout the years to come.

The money he earned he divided into two parts, some to buy a new supply of gum for the next day's work, but always a quarter or fifty cents for the gas meter at home. That money bought him light to read by, alone, secretly, after ten o'clock, when he should have been asleep but could not keep away from his books.

If the day was oppressively hot, he might steal some time to cool off in the Third Street swimming tank, a pool created right off the pier in the East River by a large wooden hoop lowered into the water. This facility was so mobbed that each of the kids was limited to fifteen minutes in the water, at which time a whistle was blown to clear the tank. Those swimmers who were dilatory about climbing out got whacked on the shank by the lifeguard's bamboo pole. Evan, already an excellent swimmer, used to duck under the water and hold his breath until the whistle signaled a new allotment of kids to leap in.

Nearer to home, Evan played in Tompkins Square Park. Many an afternoon he ran to the gazebo there, known as Nathan Straus's gazebo, where the unusual treat of cool sterilized milk was being dispensed to the children of the area. Nathan Straus's sanitary reform had a tremendous impact, because until this time, uninspected, unpasteurized milk, often from infected cows living in the city's filthy dairies, carried germs that caused diarrhea and other diseases, especially among the youngest children of the ghetto. All his life Evan was deeply grateful to Nathan Straus. Years later, through the twists of time and fate, he was able to express his appreciation when he became godfather to two of Straus's great-grandchildren.

Meanwhile, Evan's education was progressing from Longfellow's *Song of Hiawatha* to Shakespeare's *Julius Caesar*. At age eleven, he played the role of Marc Antony in a school production. To this day, he is able to recite Marc Antony's Act Three, Scene Two oration over Caesar's body. However, this first exposure to Shakespeare left an impression that went far deeper. By studying this role, and in particular this speech, he was able to discover for himself yet another lesson in the power of language. For, by the time Antony is through, by the time he pulls the rent and bloody mantle from Caesar's body and points to that "unkindest cut of all," by then, though he calls Brutus yet again an honorable man, we know that Marc Antony has utterly convinced the Roman mob that Brutus is dishonorable, and they will follow Antony anywhere he leads. Evan not only took from this experience a love of theater and the dramatic gesture, which would grow along with him, he also learned that words can do far more than sell chewing gum. Rightly timed and spoken words, he realized, have the power to sway people's thinking. When, years later and a world away in East Hampton, Evan stood up to speak and helped to defeat the introduction of convenience stores into town, it is not hard to imagine that inside the eighty-year-old civic activist the eleven-year-old "Antony" was still brilliantly cajoling, "Friends, Romans, countrymen, lend me your ears."

The following year, when he was twelve, Evan was *bar mitzvah*ed. Why at age twelve and not the usual thirteen? Evan explained, "The orthodox provision was that since as an orphan you had to depend on yourself earlier, therefore you had to go through with the ceremony a year earlier. So I became a man at age twelve! I was *bar mitzvah*ed, however, without even a celebration. They didn't spend $50,000 on me the way some families do today! They spent maybe five bucks for a little buffet consisting of sponge cake and a bottle of the cheapest 'bronf' you could get! And it wasn't even in a synagogue, but in a loft building, at Fourth Street and Avenue D, which was really still a sweatshop because the congregation hadn't yet collected enough contributions to have a proper place. The service started at seven in the morning, and I certainly didn't make any speech. The worshippers didn't want to hear from me; they had to be at work by eight. Only Father was there and one or two brothers. Of course, I was called to the Torah, and went through the motions, reciting the blessings and prayers. That was it!"

Evan was not the first, nor will he be the last, *bar mitzvah* boy for whom the ceremony turned out to be somewhat less than as advertised. However, Meshulam ben Abraham Frankel, who was going by the name Emmanuel in public school, was now an adult within the Jewish community of faith. Though he at times might seem to wander far afield, he was profoundly — and now officially — attached to Jewish life, and he would never leave it.

Evan's life from the end of grade school through high school was increasingly peripatetic. As he got older, he found jobs that took him farther and farther from the Lower East Side. He delivered flowers for Carrampas, a Greek whose store was next to Aaron's on Second Avenue at St. Mark's Place. Once Evan brought a whole armful of roses from Carrampas onto the elevated train that then ran at St. Mark's Place. Getting off at the harbor, ferrying across to Staten Island, he boarded a small locomotive train, finally arriving breathless but in time for a wedding taking place in the little Polish farming community of Bulls Head. Evan was recruited to drink some vodka and to toast the bride. He also got a phenomenal fifty cent tip, which he tucked away along with the discovery that he liked the Polish farmers. (After all, he was Polish himself.) He would find many others to talk to when he walked their lands with them, in another thirty years, in East Hampton.

Evan also worked with some of his Kleinfeld cousins taking care of the horses and wagons of Uncle Isaac's Okay Ice Cream Company. Uncle Isaac continued to be a role model for

Evan at a time when he was moving decidedly away from what he saw as the limitations of his father's devoutly religious world. Uncle Isaac had, quite by accident, given Evan the opportunity to learn about horses and riding, a sport that would become for Evan another sustaining lifelong interest.

Evan's adolescent heart was full of literature and Nature, love and poetry, horses and expansive scenery, but his experience, increasingly, was of business. He sought, especially in summer jobs, however, to combine his interests. He always found work, as he had on the Williamsburg Bridge, by the water, and among people who were having a good time.

By age fifteen, he had grown particularly close to his brother Phil — nine years his senior — who was then working in the toy department of Wanamaker's Department Store. It was a wonderful place for a boy to have his older brother employed. For years Phil not only showered gifts on his younger siblings, but he generously shared with Evan and his other brothers whatever breaks and opportunities came his way.

Evan, of course, was already making his own opportunities. He took a summer job on an excursion boat out of the Battery, calling at places whose enticing and colorful names became permanently etched in Evan's memory: Atlantic Highlands, Sea Bright, Locust Valley, Fair Haven, and Red Bank, New Jersey. As a candy butcher, Evan sold peanuts and popcorn, but the best part was calling out in a voice as booming as he could make it, "Get your Runcle's, Get your Uncle Runcle's Candy Bar."

Simply to sell what was given to him, however, wasn't challenging enough, so Evan conceived a new twist: "I decided that on each trip I would also peddle a $5 box of Whitman's chocolates. So I set it up as a kind of lottery among the passengers. People could buy as many lottery tickets as they wanted for twenty-five cents each, and then, toward the end of the cruise, there'd be a drawing and a winner. It was a great event aboard the excursion ship, and I made $25."

Evan was also excelling in school. He went briefly to Stuyvesant High School and then tested into DeWitt Clinton, a huge red brick and limestone building located at 59th Street and Tenth Avenue. Straight away, he was elected secretary of the student organization. He was getting to know lots of people, and the atmosphere was highly congenial and literary. Feeling right at home, Evan came under the particular influence of one English teacher, Joseph V. McKee, who must have been impressive indeed — and in a number of ways — for he went on to become mayor of New York City in 1932.

Meanwhile, although Evan continued to conduct himself with the filial devotion expected of him, a certain tension had entered into his relationship with his father, occasioned in part because Abish had remarried. While Jewish Law sanctioned and even encouraged this, Evan's Law, the law of the young child's emotions, did not. On one afternoon — perhaps on many — when Evan's father caught him with a volume of Tennyson on his lap and in flat-footed ignorance of some Jewish matter Abish considered essential, he yelled at his son, "Jivan, Jivan" — the pejorative for Polish "peasant."

Evan was at this time still "Emmanuel," and he was tired of the name. Since grade school, friends had shortened it to "Manny." And "Manny," apart from having little to do with Meshulam, simply did not have the appropriate ring and heft that Evan's Americanization warranted. Was not this "Jivan," in sound anyway, close to the English "Evan"? Since his father was lately calling him "peasant" anyway, Evan, the irony never lost on him, began to sign his name in high school, "Evan Manning (from Emmanuel/Manny) Frankel." To his sisters and brothers, however, he was still affectionately Meshulam, and to the growing chorus of nephews and nieces he remained Uncle Manny.

In 1918, at age sixteen, Evan graduated from high school. During the years he went to DeWitt Clinton, he had often hung his hat in the homes of his sisters in Borough Park or in other enclaves where they and their growing families lived. Now all that changed. For the first time, Evan got his own place to live, and took on a roommate, Joe Lang, a student at Columbia Law School. Evan now set his sights high, on Columbia College, from where he, too, might go to Columbia Law School. He was told, however, that he was too young to be admitted to Columbia, and also far too poor.

The place to go was, of course, City College, for a year of what Evan called "seasoning." Irving, Abish Frankel's other scholarly heir, had preceded Evan to City College, and for both boys the 135th Street campus was a heady and intellectually exciting experience. Evan enrolled in the general course, and also, presciently, took a year of draftsmanship. He, however, was also drawn to the fraternity crowd on campus. Since he was now a tall, exceptionally well-spoken young man, with a high forehead and movie star good looks likely to attract lots of girls, the Tau Delta Phi boys at City College felt very lucky when Evan Manning Frankel decided to join their house.

Evan enjoyed all aspects of college life, including rooting for the City College Beavers at sporting events. One of the Tau Delta Phi boys had a cousin, a Jewish fellow named Willie

Ball, who was one of the more bruising forwards on the varsity basketball team. Perhaps because he was, as the rules of that era required, the designated foul shooter for the entire team, Willie tended to try to incur a few fouls. Sometimes, in the process, he mixed it up with the opposing players, regardless of their size and, as Evan recalled, "he really threw a few guys on their rear ends." Evan was evidently not alone in the glee he experienced at watching Willie Ball's fearless style, for this was an era when, although tuition was now free, a Jewish quota was still in effect, and there was, as a result, a relatively small percentage of Jews at City College. The entire graduating class of 1913 numbered 209. Among them were twenty-three Eastern European Jews, a small percentage, considering the Jewish population of the city was nearly a third of the total 3.4 million inhabitants. If sports is on some level a metaphor for social and business life, Willie Ball's aggressive performances must have been heartening for the Jewish students. It is no wonder that in 1925, when Evan launched his own business, he picked Beaver forward Willie Ball as his accountant.

Evan's first year at CCNY coincided with the end of the first World War and a continuing national manpower shortage. As a fortunate consequence, Evan and a number of lucky City College students were excused from examinations in May 1919 and recruited to work in the Hudson River Valley on one of the government's model dairy farms at Highland, New York.

Early each morning, Evan went to the silo and mixed up an appetizing trough full of hot bran mash for the calves, but when his tasks were done there was much more to savor. The students were under the supervision of a City College instructor who took them to visit with John Burroughs at his famous estate in nearby Esopus, New York. Here Evan and the other students met not only the famous naturalist, who was then near the end of his life, but other visiting luminaries like Henry Ford and Thomas Alva Edison. Evan was surely not alone among the bright young CCNY city slickers whom Burroughs — wearing the mantle of Henry David Thoreau — set to dreaming about open space and that they, too, might one day enjoy land, gardens, and rural estates like this one.

In the following school year, 1919–20, Evan transferred to New York University, Washington Square campus, where he had been granted a scholarship. The aim was still to prepare to get into Columbia. Although he liked the literary and bohemian excitement of Greenwich Village, he could not linger after classes because, as always, he had to be at one job or another evenings and weekends. Evan, in this regard, was representative of most Jewish students of the time, who came from economically strapped backgrounds. Seventy-five percent of them had summer jobs and more than half held jobs during the school year — this in spite of scholarships at schools like NYU and the lack of any tuition charge at City College.

At this time, Evan's stipend for New York University was delayed for some reason, and his job as a tutor-caretaker for a young boy was not paying enough. Prizing his independence, Evan was fiercely determined not to go to any of his brothers for a loan. Perhaps he might have asked Phil for help, but Phil was working for Wanamaker's in Milwaukee. So Evan went, finally, where everybody went, to the Hebrew Free Loan Society, which would lend money, interest free, usually to help pay rent. The loan was repayable within a year. One of the significant financial institutions in the immigrants' world, the Hebrew Free Loan Society was the brainchild of the great German-Jewish banker and philanthropist Jacob Schiff. To young men of the ghetto, like Evan, who might be considering a career in business, Jacob Schiff was a particularly admirable figure, even a noble one. His many achievements, such as the financing of the expansion of the railroads, were legendary, as were his other quieter endeavors. In 1902, the year of Evan's birth, Schiff had given a seminal gift to establish Adas Israel, the synagogue in Sag Harbor, on the North Fork just above East Hampton. In some sixty years, a handful of families from that congregation, feeling it was time for the Hamptons on the South Fork to have their own synagogue, would come to Evan Frankel to help make their new temple possible.

In 1920 when the Hebrew Free Loan was coming due, Evan needed $100 to repay Jacob Schiff. Since his NYU stipend had again been delayed, he was forced to ask Aaron to repay the loan for him. His oldest brother was happy to do so. By this time, Aaron had been able to buy a weekend and summer cottage at the then uncrowded and very fashionable resort of Rockaway Beach, where Evan also came to visit and swim when work and school allowed.

Although no longer at City College in the summer of 1920, Evan signed on again to work with the fellows he had been with at Highland, New York, the previous year. This time he got one of the choice jobs, as supervisor-timekeeper on a shade-tobacco plantation in the Connecticut River Valley, midway between Hartford and Springfield. The plantation grew expensive tobacco leaf for cigar wrappers. Evan lived in the superintendent's house and rode on horseback through the fields, past mile upon mile of tobacco plants covered by cheesecloth. Toward the end of the fist work week, as the time to pay the tobacco pickers approached, Evan strapped a Colt automatic revolver onto his belt, entered the barn with some trepidation, and practiced — presumably for the first time — the art of shooting. When the paymaster arrived, Evan, armed, mounted, and dangerous, accompanied him on his tour of the plantation as he paid the pickers.

The Tau Delta Phi boys, some of whom had been with him that summer, said good-humoredly that Evan had bossed everyone around. But to his family, Evan described the experience somewhat differently. "Imagine," he told them, "I was riding a horse. I was a gentleman!" To all his family, Evan was proving himself a *wunderkind,* and Columbia College, and thereafter Columbia Law, could not be too far off.

To bring it nearer, Evan, in the fall of 1920, moved up to the Morningside Heights-Columbia University neighborhood. He lived in the Zeta Beta Tau fraternity house on 114th Street because Tau Delta Phi did not have a house at Columbia. However, without working, there was no way he could afford the $300 Columbia tuition.

There was another reason for Evan's reluctance to become a full-time student at this stage of his life. The world of work, interesting work at which he was proving he could be successful, beckoned. The result for Evan in 1920 was, as he recalled, real conflict: "One of the jobs I had was as a guide at the Commodore Hotel. It had just opened up, on 42nd Street, and it was the last word in hotels. I remember the wonderful interior architecture, and a Renaissance ceiling. I was required, as a bright college boy, to spout to the different groups of tourists and visitors as they came through. I supplemented the guide work by being in charge of the hat-check concession. After a while, the guy who owned it wanted to make me a partner. It was a lucrative thing, but of course I didn't accept. My sights were high. I didn't want to be a partner in a hat check! I wanted to go to Columbia Law School.

"On the other hand, since I was working and making money, as I looked ahead to all that schooling, it seemed like an awfully long time to wait. I wanted to get there fast. I wanted to get out into the world."

The conflict was to be partially resolved in 1925 when Evan launched his business, but not definitively until 1933 when the business really took off. All during those years, Evan harbored a yearning for the halls of academe and a poetic-creative urge that would give the business style he was developing a very distinctive literary-theatrical panache.

In the meantime, however, he worked at the Commodore and other places downtown, returning to Columbia each evening to take extension courses. After class, he sat on the steps of the ZBT house with his fraternity friends, flirting with the pretty nurses as they walked past on 114th Street bound for the evening shift at St. Luke's Hospital.

The 1920s was an economically expansive decade. By 1922, Phil had left Wanamaker's, returned to New York, and married his sweetheart Debbie. Since his father-in-law was a partner in Mangel's Stores, Phil went to work for the women's apparel chain. Dozens of new shops were being planned nationally, and Phil was beginning to take charge of coordinating the construction. He was in a position to help his brothers. Irving went to work for Mangel's. He would eventually go on to become a district manager. But Evan was studying to be lawyer, was he not? Phil probably knew his baby brother better than anyone in the family, and he appreciated his talents and his quiet dilemma. If Evan, as Phil suspected, had thoughts of a career in business percolating beneath the legal aspirations, would not some real experience in business and sales — the real stuff and not hat checking — help him to make up his mind?

Phil learned that Paramount Contracting Company, which was building some Mangel's stores, was in need of a sales representative. He knew just the young man to suggest — a handsome twenty-year-old student, smart as a whip, who spoke better than his professors and who could charm your socks off!

Phil encouraged Evan to apply. Evan did, and he immediately got the job. Being a salesman still allowed him sufficient control over his schedule so that he could continue to take courses at Columbia in the afternoon and early evening. Evan, who was such a whiz kid many thought he was no mere employee but the son of the owner, became a tremendous asset to Paramount. The owner did, indeed, have his eye on Evan for a major promotion. But another Paramount employee, Isaac Ross, a master carpenter and cabinetmaker, had an eye on Evan, too, and would soon make him a business proposal that would change his life.

First came the summer of 1922. For years now, summers had been for Evan, as they are in Nature, the season for growth. It was a time to find, even though he was poor, some opportunity to get away, to travel, or to have some new experience, preferably in a rural or pelagic setting, where he could, by reaching beyond himself, expand and change.

He might have spent the time in intense preparation to matriculate into Columbia, or pursuing his success at Paramount Contracting. But Evan, who was already extraordinarily adept at listening to the beat of his own drummer, said to himself, "I may go into business and I may go into the law, but whatever I become, I am going to be, above all, a Gentleman. And a Gentleman must see the Continent!"

The question, of course, was: How could a poor Lower East Side boy afford the grand tour?

Enter a well-to-do Columbia classmate and Evan's sister Frieda. The friend's father was a maritime entrepreneur who had bought the SS *Philadelphia*, an 1898 merchant ship, and transformed her into a passenger vessel that, in the summer of 1922, was chartered to take a beautiful cargo of American college girls on their grand tour. Evan's friend told him there was room for a "crew" of about eight boys to help out around the ship as she made her ports-of-call along the Mediterranean coast.

One can imagine how eager Evan and his friend must have been to study the glory that was Greece and the grandeur that was Rome, particularly in the company of half the girls of Randolph Macon College. Since all Evan needed now to get him launched was a little capital, he made his case to his sister Frieda, who pawned some jewelry and staked him to $300. Such, anyway, is the Frankel family tale. At a Passover *seder* thirty years later, when Evan and Frieda were kidding each other about whether he had repaid the loan, Evan calculated that if he hadn't, he owed his sister, including interest, at least $120,000.

In June 1922, the SS *Philadelphia* made her Atlantic crossing with "Cadet Navigator" Evan Frankel aboard. One night, as he stood his lonely four-hour watch in the crow's-nest, an exceedingly narrow platform high above the deck, a bold young woman climbed the ratlines and squeezed in to keep Evan company. The ship was moving along the coast of Portugal, bound for Gibraltar, when Evan, passionately involved, glimpsed lights on the horizon. As per regulations, he hollered out, "Lights on the starboard!" There was dead silence from the quartermaster at the wheel. Evan hollered again. More silence. The girl hid behind the mast as finally the quartermaster screamed from the deck below, "Goddammit, you landlubber, that's not starboard!" And he threatened to climb up to teach this Lothario of a cadet navigator the difference between starboard and port. To this day, Evan insists he did know port from starboard but had been temporarily distracted by the affectionate embraces of his surprise guest.

The entire voyage on the increasingly unseaworthy SS *Philadelphia* was a comedy of exciting mishaps. She had to lay up in Gibraltar for repairs. The refrigeration went bad, followed quickly by the food. Then the engines didn't work properly, but there were no facilities at Gibraltar to fix them. The ship proceeded to Naples for repairs, giving Evan an opportunity to see Pompeii and Herculaneum in the company of his pal and a CCNY teacher. Then they went to Rome just in time to see black-shirted Mussolini parade up the Via Veneto beneath Fascist flags on his way to be sworn in as premier of Italy. Meanwhile, the Chilean stokers on the SS *Philadelphia* mutinied because they were not being paid. Without funds to pay for crew or repairs, the ship could not sail on to Alexandria. "So we stayed in Italy," Evan remembered, "totally stuck, strike-bound, mired, and having the greatest time!" When the United States government finally put all the passengers on another ship, Evan cabled his brother Irving for funds. When the money came, toward the end of August, Evan was able to go home.

III

In the fall of 1922, Evan still had one foot at Columbia and one at Paramount Contracting, and he continued to bestride his future. A rapid self-teacher, and now European traveler, he impressed his college friends with his worldliness, and his business friends with his scholarliness. He still felt very much in conflict, but he was beginning to fashion out of both worlds an inimitable personal style.

Evan continued to harbor the dream of the law in 1923, even when, at the age of twenty-one, he was made a precocious vice-president of Paramount Contracting. But it was going to take more than a title to hold him, for Evan by now knew that he was a "supersalesman." And if he could do such a superlative job working for Paramount part time, why could he not do the same, even better, working for himself full time?

Such was one of the arguments Isaac Ross made to Evan in 1925, when Isaac proposed they both leave Paramount and form, as equal partners, a business of their own. Ross was not only an excellent carpenter, he was also an astute businessman. A Russian Jew, considerably older than Evan, with a pronounced Old World accent, he realized that if he hitched his skilled craftsmanship to the rising star of Evan Frankel's salesmanship, they might have an unbeatable business combination. Nor did it escape Ross that the man who commissioned work for Mangel's Stores was Evan Frankel's brother Philip.

On the other hand, in spite of this advantageous associaton and Evan's indisputable sales acumen, Isaac Ross wanted proof of Evan's seriousness. He did not want to take on as a partner someone who might, in six months, suddenly quit in order to go to law school. Ross would not take Evan without the evidence of genuine commitment, which, in Ross's thinking, would take the form of a $3,000 investment of capital.

A moment of decision had arrived for Evan. In what had become a characteristic ability to look not at detail, but at the "Big Picture," Evan did not quibble about the money. It was a fortune, but he believed he could find it. More importantly, he was required to assess his innermost direction. When he did, he realized that at heart he was not a student, but an autodidact. Moreover, to go into business was not to forsake learning, but rather to pursue it through different means — through cultivation of his interest in people, through continuing self-learning and self-mastery, and through travel. Indeed, he might be able to earn enough some years down the road to pay for the full-time college and legal — or was it literary? — education that he could not afford now. At this crossroads, Evan's decision was that of the vast majority of the Eastern European immigrant generation and their children who recognized that educational accomplishment would be more the consequence of success in business than its cause.

Without delay Evan borrowed $1,000 from his brother Phil's father-in-law, $1,000 from a partner in Mangel's, and $1,000 from Mayer's father-in-law, owner of the successful Steinberg's Dairy Restaurant. Evan promised to repay the loan to each at the end of a year, so confident was he that the business would be a success.

But not everyone in the Frankel family was so confident or altogether pleased with Evan's decision. Although Evan's father had been relatively silent about the direction of his son's life and had not spoken of all the hope and promise he had invested in the youngest and most scholarly of his boys, Abish Frankel held fire no longer. "Carpentry! Cabinets! Office design! Store fixtures!" he cried in Yiddish. "What kind of job is *that* for a Jewish boy?" Evan's riposte was a humdinger, not only in the tales of the Frankels but in all the annals of father-son face-offs, for he said to his orthodox father, "Jesus of Nazareth was a carpenter, and he was Jewish!"

Not only was Evan not to be deterred, but the youthful bravado of his humor revealed another facet of Evan's Americanization that was already in place at age twenty-three: an ironic delight in confounding expectations that there might be limits to where a bright young Jewish fellow could go. Evan was going precisely where he wanted. In 1925, the year F. Scott Fitzgerald published *The Great Gatsby*, his exploration of the American Dream, Evan Frankel launched his own dream by establishing Ross Frankel, Incorporated, designers of "distinctive interiors and unusual fronts" for stores and offices. With hardly more capital than Evan had been able to scrounge together through his loans, Ross Frankel opened for business on 40th Street in midtown Manhattan.

At first the firm consisted of Evan, Isaac Ross, and a secretary, all in one small office. Phil, who was Mangel's Stores head of real estate, made certain his company would be Ross Frankel's first client. But soon there were more. In the very beginning, without a factory, Evan and Isaac Ross limited their work to design. Evan made calls on potential clients, and in the absence of a staff of draftsmen and architects, he discovered in himself a facility for design. He had not only innate good taste, but, more importantly, the ability to imagine in its totality the atmosphere the client wanted. Moreover, once Evan sensed the general environment, he could help clients articulate the detail. So the clients, with good reason, felt Evan had helped them midwife their own ideas into reality. Back at the office, Ross — and later a team of architects and draftsmen — would take Evan's design ideas and turn them into drawings, which Evan then presented to the client for approval. In this manner the business grew, and one year from the day he borrowed $3,000, Evan, with characteristic theatricality, called seriatim on his three lenders, giving each a check for $1,060, the principal plus six percent interest.

By the end of 1926, Evan had built up the business so successfully that Ross Frankel was not only designing, but — through subcontractors under Isaac Ross's supervision — the new company was completely fabricating interiors and storefronts. The burden of coordinating carpenters, electricians, and other craftsmen was such that the firm decided to open its own factory. The move was made to expanded office space, with a large factory behind, at 402 West 27th Street.

Here, with a sense of economy — he abhorred wasting a single panel of wood — and with Germanic efficiency, Isaac Ross presided over a growing shop. In the new space, Evan's bailiwick grew even larger. Not only did Evan bring in all the business virtually on his own, but he supervised the daily office operations, the finances, and every facet outside the factory. Evan also helped to create the concept for a highly popular and distinctive ultra-modern storefront. Then he promoted, marketed, and sold that concept all over the Eastern seaboard.

As the business grew, the Ross Frankel team was rounded out with the addition of architect Morris Lapidus, a Columbia University graduate, whom Evan hired in the late 1920s.

"Morris Lapidus," Evan recalled, "was an exceedingly able guy and the principal architect for us in the early days, especially for the Mangel's Stores. He helped us become known for our storefronts right away.

"Up to that time, a storefront consisted of two windows on the sidewalk and a door in the middle flush next to them, and that was that. We started the arcade storefront that went way back from the sidewalk. To walk into the store you had to go past these two large show windows and along an entryway set back from the street. The more opportunity we made for custsomers to look at merchandise before entering the store, the more they would buy when they went inside. At the time the idea was considered very newfangled."

Ross Frankel, after pioneering the arcade storefront, began to prefabricate them, load them on trains, and deliver them to Mangel's and other retail stores throughout the Northeast. The quality of the work, the design, the materials, and the on-time delivery had, by the end of five years' operation, put Ross Frankel into the front ranks in its field. Even in an era of rapid economic growth, the rise of Ross Frankel from a dream in 1925 to a prestigious national firm by 1929 was by any measure a real business phenomenon. Certainly the competition thought so!

One's life at work is rarely entirely separate from one's private life, and Evan's early business credo was that he did not do business with people he would not also invite to dinner. Since Evan found most of humankind fascinating, people liked him tremendously in return, and his business and social circles interlocked and expanded. For example, Evan frequented Briarcliff Lodge in Westchester County north of New York City, where he was a much-in-demand waltzer. Evan explained: "Briarcliff was a very posh hotel, one of the best in New York, in immediate proximity to the Pocantico Hills estate of the Rockefellers. Way back in 1927, when we were just starting out in business, I got a job on the weekends waltzing with the ladies whose husbands didn't waltz. These were Saturday night dances, and all the guests were very accomplished and very conservative people, often heads of corporations. So I used to live at Briarcliff in the summers and commute to New York City. It was a beautiful drive up the Saw Mill River Parkway. I drove a Packard I had just bought, and evenings and weekends I had the greatest time. The job enabled me to live like a lord at a minimum price, and I began many friendships and business contacts."

Evan rode often in Central Park with his Columbia friends, and some evenings he gathered with a group of young men to play poker and drink perhaps a jigger of bootleg, Prohibition-era whiskey. At one such poker evening, in the card room of a brownstone on the Upper West Side, Evan was introduced to an elegant young fellow named J. Emerson Thors. Emerson at the time was beginning to work his way up through the Kuhn Loeb banking firm. An amateur artist, he was from an English family of honored Royal Academicians. A second new friend was handsome and witty John Small, who also worked on Wall Street, and who, like Emerson, had an artistic background. John's sister, Hannah, and her husband Eugene Ludens were both accomplished painters who moved in the circle of Alfred Stieglitz and Georgia O'Keeffe.

Evan saw himself mirrored in both Emerson and John: young men of exceptional personal style, who were on their way to being business successes, young men who also recognized that business success would not suffice unless it gave them the opportunity to express themselves creatively. Evan, Emerson, and John became close friends. All three shared a passionate love for theater and for women. Since it was easier and far less expensive to afford the former, they often went like the Three Musketeers down Broadway to the theater. During the week, Emerson sent out invitations, illustrated by his own drawings, and Evan, John Small, and sometimes other friends met at the theater door. The plays were often first-rate and the tickets then still easily affordable. Afterwards, they went to Frankie and Johnny's or some other speakeasy where the writers and journalists and the Harvard, Yale, and Columbia crowd gathered. Or the three might go to the Blue Ribbon, a Swiss restaurant on West 44th Street, perhaps to discuss Paul Robeson in O'Neill's *The Emperor Jones*, deliberating whether it was his voice, his acting, or his stature and his blackness that made his performance so memorable.

John fell in love and married early. His nineteen-year-old wife, Amy, was a sculptor and also an excellent cook. At the Smalls' table, where Evan dined often, he learned about art. In addition, Evan developed from Emerson a great fondness for things British. Evan had the actor's gift — a superb memory, a quick grasp, and the remarkable ability rapidly to make something new completely his own. He combined this with a fine talent for choosing friends. In the Smalls' company, he enjoyed himself precisely because he was also learning and growing with them.

With two other friends Evan took an apartment at 10 West 73rd Street in Manhattan. The bachelor quarters featured an unusually luxurious bathroom, with glass ceilings, massage table, steam box, and reducing machine. A strategically placed mirror on one wall made it possible to view occupants of the shower stall. Although Evan denies he ever observed his female guests' ablutions, Emerson Thors suggested that there is a "convenient gap in Evan's memory. Many girls used to come over," Emerson recalled, with a smile, "to avail themselves of Evan's facilities!"

And there were many women in Evan's life. "He was handsome as Heathcliff," Amy Small remembered, "so I went out of my way to tell each of Evan's girlfriends to have a good time, but not expect a proposal."

Evan was not ready to settle down, as John Small had and as Emerson did in 1929, when he fell madly in love with a French girl, Chou Chou. Emerson married her as fast as he could, a marriage that was to last until Chou Chou's death fifty-one years later. Evan wasn't ready to settle down because he was still too busy cultivating the art of friendship. "Friendship," Emerson Thors said, comparing the era in which he met Evan with today, "is a word equally as profound as love. And love is one of the most misused words I know!"

IV

The late 1920s were wild, heady days. In his Packard, open even in winter, Evan used to drive regularly up to Briarcliff Lodge with his friends. More often than not, he had a blonde beside him for warmth, and in the rumble seat behind sat the Thorses wrapped in their heavy coats, with the icicles, Evan remembered, bristling in Emerson's mustache!

Lael Tucker Wertenbaker, who has written sixteen books since then, was an exuberant eighteen-year-old playwright in 1928 when she dated Evan. She remembers him well, and offered a glimpse not only of Evan-in-formation, but an era too: "I belonged to a more raffish crowd than Evan, but he liked creative people, and he really did stand out. Always stylishly dressed in a Brooks Brothers suit, he was careful about his manners and his clothes. Although most of the people I knew thought prejudice was stupid, there was a good deal of 'cheerful anti-Semitism.' Nothing ugly, however. Evan never announced his Jewishness, but one was aware of it. I'm not sure, but perhaps he was a little aloof for that reason, until he was sure of an amiable, friendly attitude.

"My impression was that Evan was very literate, but with perhaps an uncertain accent. Maybe he wasn't sure of it. After all, I was busy dropping my own Southern accent in New York! The 1920s were a playful time. The Lunts were our heroes, along with the Fitzgeralds, and everybody was busy doing their own happy inventing, and all young people — and we were young! — presented an image."

In addition to a widening social circle, Evan, as the 1920s drew to a close, found himself busier than ever as an uncle. He drove his long right-hand-drive Packard into the lives of his nieces and nephews, a role model for them as Uncle Isaac had been for him. Evan's emotional attachment to his nieces and nephews was also very strong. Evan's youth and his own loss of a parent gave him an empathy for children and a feeling for the vulnerability of a child's world, which he has continued to communicate to all the children he has come in contact with throughout a lifetime.

Evan hired a number of his nieces and nephews, such as Frieda's son David and Annie Gross's son Herman, to work for him after school at Ross Frankel. He set up special annual outings — trips to the theater or to Barnum and Bailey's circus, for example — with each of his brothers' and sisters' kids. The outings were highly anticipated, glamorous, memorable events in their lives. When Irving moved to North Carolina, Evan kept in touch with his nephews there, sending books, theater tickets, and an open invitation to visit so they might see all of New York from the wonderful rumble seat of his Packard. At the many family gatherings and Jewish holidays, especially the Passover *seder* at either Annie's or Frieda's house, Uncle Manny was always the cynosure, an eye-opening experience for children who saw him as a traveler from exciting places that they, too, might one day visit.

First, however, they — and everyone else — had to weather the Great Depression.

By the time the Crash came, in October 1929, Ross Frankel had become successful enough for Evan to move to the penthouse apartment at 5 Riverside Drive. This apartment, which was to be Evan's New York City headquarters for the next forty years, had a one-hundred-foot wraparound terrace and large floor-to-ceiling windows. From there Evan could see the Schwab mansion, the Hudson River, and the spectacular new George Washington Bridge. With the windows always open, fresh air streaming in, and the heart uplifted by the changing panoramic river views, Evan had fashioned for himself not only a dwelling as far "out" of Manhattan as one can be while still being in it, but also a refuge from the dislocations and despair the Depression was about to usher in.

Although Ross Frankel had grown dramatically between 1926 and the Crash, its future was now by no means certain. In 1929 there were fifty people working in the shop under Isaac Ross's supervision — mechanics, carpenters, cabinetmakers — and that number, depending on the volume of business, sometimes soared to one hundred. Still, almost all the accounts were generated by Evan alone, so in that sense Ross Frankel was a one-man business, or a business in which one man left his stamp on all facets of the operation. Evan could not afford now to let his efforts flag.

Not an aggressively hard-sell salesman, but a charmingly forceful one, Evan continued to do what he did best. This consisted of going directly to the top decision-makers in a company, meeting them either on neutral, social turf like the Briarcliff Lodge (where he was now not a hired waltzer, but an always welcomed regular guest) or entertaining them himself at 5 Riverside Drive. There, Evan's growing collection of the English classics — usually in first edition — or the novelty of his player piano, or a delicious meal prepared by his cook Pauline could turn a potential customer into both a patron and a friend. "I steeped myself in people," Evan said, "in people and not just in my business. So, when people flocked around me, connections were made, and the business naturally flourished."

However, could a distinctive product sold by one man's great personal charm be sufficient in the face of mounting business bankruptcies and the belly-up economy of the early 1930s? At the beginning of the Depression, the Mangel's Stores account, which had launched Ross Frankel, helped carry it through. Prior to the Crash, Mangel's and a few other retail chains had signed long-term lease agreements that, Depression or not, they had to honor. So the building of unusual storefronts — the arcade and the even newer convex design —continued to be the Ross Frankel staple. However, there was little new business on the horizon, and the horizon was where Evan was always looking. Unemployed people, from carpenters to architects, came begging for what work there was at Ross Frankel.

Although Ross Frankel's financial prospects were uncertain, Evan was doing better than many other business people, whom the Crash had brutally wiped out. In this climate, in which many people were abandoned by fair-weather friends, Evan, who was surely no stranger to hard times, came through for his family and people close to him. Amy Small remembers well: "After the Crash, when we lost absolutely everything, Evan was very good to John and me. Evan became a silent partner in my husband's firm, John Small and Company. We had every Christmas and Thanksgiving together during those hard early years, and lots more after that. Evan was very devoted to us."

There were many other kindnesses. He made loans to friends and family. He gave outright gifts. He co-signed bank loans or credit union agreements to tide over a brother's struggling business. Perhaps this generosity and concern grew out of his memories of childhood. Perhaps it reflected the example set by Phil, whom Evan admired so completely and who had been so kind to him. Whatever the reason, it became known in the Frankel family that support for those who needed it could always be found at Uncle Evan's door. "He might fill your ear with what a fool you were to get into a jam," said Evan's nephew, seventy-three-year-old David Plesser, "but his family loyalties were profound, and we always admired him."

Evan was particularly involved with the family of Annie Gross, his oldest sister. She was eighteen years his senior, and had been *in loco parentis* since 1910, when their mother died. Now, twenty years later, in 1930, as the gloom of the Depression was settling over the land, Annie's husband suddenly died. She was left with six growing boys to care for, and only a fledgling insurance business to support them all. Evan was close to these nephews: Jess, Harold, Nathan, Seymour, Herman, and Aaron. He shared a special bond with them, not only because he, at twenty-eight, was a very young uncle (Annie's oldest, Jess, was barely six years younger), but also because Evan felt deeply grateful to Annie. Orthodox, loving, caring, fiercely devoted to family, she had assumed, over the years, the larger role of matriarch and the Jewish Conscience of the Frankel family.

Evan took an obligation seriously, and whether it was financial or emotional, he was uncomfortable until it was repaid. Struck by the similarity between his own childhood loss of a parent and what the Gross children now faced, Evan let Annie know he would help her in any way he could. He was particularly admiring and supportive of Jess, who rose to the occasion and took over what was left of his father's insurance agency.

Evan directed business Jess's way, and eventually the agency grew so that three other Gross boys went into it as well.

Of all the Gross children, the one Evan devoted himself to most was the fourth son, Seymour, who, as a result of a childhood accident, had become deaf and mute. Evan told Annie that she needn't worry about Seymour's education, and arranged for him to have the best training possible at the Lexington School for the Deaf, in Manhattan. Evan was keen on Seymour's learning skills that would help him in life, and, when he came of age, made a place for him at Ross Frankel. It wasn't only money Evan invested in Seymour. It was time and concern and companionship. Anxious to be able to communicate better, Evan taught himself signing and spent many hours, taking Seymour to the country or to the beach, establishing himself in the young man's life less as an uncle, more as an older brother or, perhaps, even an adoptive father.

By the spring of 1932, Franklin Roosevelt, Governor of New York and candidate for President, had not yet come out with a blueprint to raise the nation out of the depths of the Depression. Unemployment had reached twenty-four percent, car sales were down eighty percent since 1929. Meshulam Meyer Weisenfreund, also known as Paul Muni, was starring in *I Am a Fugitive from a Chain Gang*, a film in which the Muni character, desperately hungry for a fifteen-cent hamburger, is involved in the robbery of a diner. Times were very tough indeed.

Ross Frankel had some business, but not much. What if the Depression lingered on for years or got deeper? Evan had been in his business for seven years and was now thirty years old. He was young enough to try something utterly new and different, and considered that this might be the time to strike, to make the departure while he was still young enough and had some savings.

As he cast about trying to read the future — the nation's and his own — Evan's old ambition of Columbia College and Columbia Law School hardly seemed appealing any more. However, an older and far more cherished dream, one that he had kept a virtual secret, perhaps even from himself, now resurfaced and laid claim to his imagination. Had he not all his life loved, above all other times, the hours spent reading Shakespeare, Tennyson, Thackeray, Browning, and the other stars of English literature? Furthermore, was he not truly an Anglophile at heart? Had he not been one all his life? It was only natural that he become an English scholar! And what better time to enter the world of English studies than now, when the economy was so mired and the world of business seemed impervious to improvement? He still had some savings from the business and could subsidize his education quite nicely.

As the summer of 1932 neared, Evan spent evenings at the library reading through college catalogues and psychologically adjusting to the idea of abandoning his business. The result was that he refined his plan in a crucial way: he would not study English at City College or New York University or even Columbia, or anywhere in America for that matter. To take this major step in his life would make sense, could be justified, only if he went to study at the source itself, at Oxford or Cambridge University in England.

Ten years after his first European trip, Evan embarked on his second. He planned an itinerary that would take him through France, Germany, Austria, Hungary, and Italy, and then finally from there up to England, for the beginning of the Oxford-Cambridge phase of his life in September 1932. He kept his apartment on Riverside Drive, however, just in case. It could easily be disposed of later.

If Evan's first transatlantic passage, at age two, had been in steerage, and his second, at age twenty, had been in crew's quarters and part time in the crow's-nest with college women, this third trip was strictly first class. The rock bottom 1932 prices made deluxe affordable.

Evan traveled by himself. He was by now comfortable with this from his many business trips, and, of course, he always met people en route. On board the luxury liner he was introduced to a serious young lawyer, Harry Green, who later would build one of the largest corporate law firms in Baltimore. Nearly complete opposites in temperament, they nevertheless became good friends on the ship and, as it turned out, remained so for the next thirty years until Harry Green's death. In 1938 Evan would become a godfather to Harry Green's daughter, Harrie Ellen, with whom he would retain a special bond all his life.

In July 1932, however, after three weeks together in Cannes and Paris, Harry Green left to come home, and Evan took the train for Salzburg and its famous summer music festival, a lodestar for all visitors. Munich was directly on the way, however, so Evan decided to stop off there for just one night. That chance decision brought him a remarkable encounter with Adolph Hitler.

"After registering at the Four Seasons Hotel," Evan remembered, "I asked the clerk what I might do in Munich on a Sunday afternoon. He directed me to an open-air beer garden nearby. It was a big, crowded place. I spoke German fairly well, and the maitre d' took me to a table with four other guys my age. There was one available chair and he sat me down. I nodded to the others at the table, and then I heard them talking about me, and I gathered they were displeased with something. I said to them, in German, 'What have I done to be excused for?' They said I was a Prussian, which was a very bad thing in the eyes of these upper-middle-class Bavarians. In those days I was dressed like a real patrician, and my accent was different from theirs, possibly better.

"I said, 'I'm not a Prussian. I'm an American.' Then I summoned the waiter and ordered beer for all. Now these fellows sat up and took notice, and we began to talk. I asked what they did and they said they were going to the university. That surprised me since they were, like me, about thirty years old. I asked why and they said they stayed in school because there were no jobs. With the beer, there were only black and white radishes, nothing else to eat, so by this time they were a little drunk, and I was paying for all their beers, and we got to be drinking pals. Finally they said, 'Come on,' and I asked them where they were going, and their answer was that now I was to be *their* guest.

"We went to a rathskeller and were ushered in through an assembly room, to a stage where we sat down at a large table. Apparently there were going to be some speeches. A little later in walks this guy, and a couple of people with him. My fellows introduced me to Herr Adolph Hitler!

"Hitler didn't mean nearly as much in 1932 as he did afterwards. I didn't recognize his face, but when they told me his name, I recognized it. He'd just won a third of the votes to be Chancellor. He'd served time in prison, and he was treated as some kind of hero. Everybody stood up. He wasn't in uniform. He was wearing a suit like everyone else.

"So we shook hands and sat down. The guys I was with

had introduced me to him as a very important American. Hitler, apparently impressed, was very interested in talking to me, this very important American, but first he was going to address the crowd.

"He made his speech, which was pretty much the kind of harangue the world saw later. Who knew then what he would turn into? Afterward, my friends asked me to come upstairs to a private dining room. There I was seated right next to Herr Hitler, so he could question the 'important American.' He said something about Americans not cooperating enough with Germany. I denied it. I kept feeding him the idea that we were cooperating with Germany, and, as a matter of fact we were, not with his side of the government, but with the government of Hindenberg. He was interested, and I said over and over again that we were not enemies but rather eager to help Germany. All the questions he asked were political. I assured him we were doing a lot in America!

"His style of speaking to me personally was entirely without charm; he was simply inquisitive. Actually I wasn't impressed with Hitler at all. His suit was rumpled and he was kind of a slob. We talked about America, and he never once mentioned the Jews. He, of course, had no idea I was Jewish. He was just interested in gaining the support of someone he thought was an 'important American.' The Germans were doing that all the time then. After dinner, he departed, and my friends took me under their wing again and told me they would pick me up at eight in the morning to show me around Munich.

"Sure enough, there they were at eight the following morning. Eight sharp! They toured me around town and then to the farm of one of the guys. At day's end, they said they would come again in the morning and they kept saying how badly other countries were treating the Germans. In those days we didn't know anything about what was really happening! Finally, on the third day, I realized I had had enough. They were going to come again at eight, so I resolved to beat them at their own punctuality. I left word to be called at six; there was a train coming from Paris to Munich at seven-fifteen and bound for Salzburg, and I made sure I was on it!"

It was a great relief for Evan to arrive in Salzburg. He stayed for a week, taking in the music and the drama. The balconies of the main town square had been converted to stages, and Evan was present for the traditional and memorable medieval morality play, *Everyman*.

With letters of introduction from banking friends, Evan went on to Budapest and then Vienna and managed an introduction to Jacob Rothschild and other dignitaries. He also visited the palace of former Emperor Franz Joseph, about whom his parents and Annie had told him so much. The Depression, however, was especially bad in Vienna, and the palace was abandoned.

At the hotel in Budapest, the novelty for the well-to-do was a machine that created waves in the swimming pool. Evan stood poolside amused, when, at the sound of a bell, the hotel guests jumped in the pool to frolic in the machine-made waves. When the bell sounded again, the waves stopped and everyone climbed out. This was when Evan, perhaps remembering with some irony his childhood at the Third Street tank on the Lower East Side, dived in alone, for a little of the real swimming that he loved.

It escaped no one, least of all Evan, that this machine that made waves was an ineffectual distraction from the ubiquitous poverty. He saw in the faces of the rich, even as they waltzed, the desperate eyes of church mice. Evan had intended this part of his itinerary to be a kind of nostalgic loop through the Austro-Hungarian Empire into which he had been born in 1902, but both towns and people everywhere, drained once by war, now had their suffering compounded by the Depression. The experience was far more disturbing than sentimental.

Toward the end of August 1932, Evan went down to Venice and had some fun and his fill of swimming on the Lido. But the moment of personal reckoning was also at hand. To Oxford or not to Oxford? That was the question Evan now had to answer. Here is how he did it:

"I was still harboring thoughts of doing what I originally set out to do: go to Oxford and register at Magdalen College. I had all the catalogues with me, and I had read so much about Oxford, I felt I had already gone there! On the other hand, by this time I was tired of meeting new people all the time, and giving forth with my version of life and listening to theirs and then correcting their notions of America. I was tired of all the interplay, and then Genoa called. It was a port of departure for America, so I left Venice for Genoa and then sailed home. I was really homesick. I had discovered the place I had come from was where I wanted to be. I was both surprised and not surprised at my decision. I had a strong desire to get back to my accustomed haunts and pace, and to my business; then I also had a sense that things were going to change."

When he returned to the United States, Evan threw himself into his business with renewed determination. There had always been something about his salesmanship that was beyond salesmanship, beyond even supremely confident "supersalesmanship." It was a kind of aura energizing the atmosphere and making life around Evan more intense, somehow twice lived, or highlighted, as if on a stage. Evan tapped this talent, dedicating himself now to making what was a very fine business into an exceedingly prosperous one.

He was helped by stirrings in the economy and, in particular, by the repeal of Prohibition in 1933. Evan met socially Bill Cleland, president of Joseph E. Seagram & Sons, at the moment that firm, just re-establishing itself in the United States, was about to design and build offices on two floors recently leased in the Chrysler Building. Cleland was so impressed with the interior of a restaurant Ross Frankel had just completed on 59th Street next to the Sherry Netherland Hotel, that he hired Evan to do the new offices. But first Evan had to go to Canada to show the plans to the boss, Sam Bronfman.

They met at the Bronfmans' home in Montreal. There was some question whether Bronfman was going to approve the plans Evan had brought up. Until this meeting Bronfman didn't know that this handsome, British-sounding guy was Jewish. However, since it was Friday night, Evan volunteered to chant the *kiddush*, the blessing for the Sabbath wine. This gesture seemed to tip the balance in favor of Ross Frankel, and Sam Bronfman soon gave his okay. Evan must have felt a certain gratitude for his father's punctilious observance of the Sabbath, since thirty years later those blessings were helping him turn the corner in his business.

Evan, Isaac Ross, and Morris Lapidus threw themselves into the Seagram project. They created working areas, fixtures, a superlative set of carved wooden doors for the executive suite, and furniture, including a desk specifically designed for Sam Bronfman. The design married light, wood, and utility so effectively, the overall space created was both highly modern and richly dignified. It succeeded so well, the company gave much of their design and construction of offices and distribution facilities to Evan, and that effectively got Ross Frankel through its most critical economic moment of the Depression.

By 1934, Ross Frankel was building offices and stores for Joseph E. Seagram & Sons, Bulova Watch Company, and Doubleday Bookstores, the jobs ranging from New York City to Detroit, Chicago, and points west. Back in 1927, while the first nail was still being hammered in Ross Frankel's first storefront outside of the five boroughs, Evan had enjoyed, with youthful braggadocio, redoing the company stationary so that the logo read, "Ross Frankel/Operating Nationally." Now the company truly was. The large map in Evan's wood-paneled office, which tracked the projects across the country, proudly displayed, by the middle of the decade, fifteen shiny pushpins.

Evan was traveling more extensively than ever before — to supervise projects or to meet new people at Briarcliff Lodge, at resorts in the Bahamas, or at the Breakers in Palm Beach. These places where Evan went to make new friends or contacts, or to relax and conjure up new business were by and large watering holes of the very wealthy. In the 1930s Jewish guests were, by design, very few and far between. While Evan enjoyed the fertile combination of work and play, he never hid or denied his Jewishness, and his increasingly Anglophile taste in clothes, manners, and deportment gave him the coloration necessary for acceptance. Indeed, if he so chose, he could "out-WASP" any "WASP" within twenty miles, with spectacular effect. There was perhaps something about being the outsider inside — maybe the actor's quiet glee in the masquerade, or perhaps the pleasure of spoiling stereotypes of Jewish style and behavior — that Evan not merely enjoyed, but to which he seemed attracted. Moreover, if a new acquaintance realized that this remarkable young man, in addition to being witty and bright and a good horseman, was also Jewish — and perhaps the first Jewish fellow he'd met socially — Evan's attractiveness and his unusual aura were, in this manner, magnified. To be always familiar and yet always surprising — and absolutely never dull — was one reason why such a wide range of people were then, and still are, drawn to Evan.

In Evan's talks with these company executives whom he met and eventually built for, he learned that the smartest business people in the mid-1930s were taking out long-term leases while prices were still at Depression lows. This was not only good for Ross Frankel; it was also an early and fundamental real estate lesson. Evan would not forget it. In time, he would leave his mark on that field, too.

As the business flourished through the 1930s, although Evan must have felt he was living a fantasy, what pleased him most was the reputation for excellence Ross Frankel had earned. The firm was building, as Evan's 1936 advertising declared, "the store of tomorrow today," but they were doing it by utilizing fine materials and workmanship for a reasonable price and by *always* delivering on schedule.

On-time delivery was a point of particular pride for Evan, especially in a field that even in the 1930s was noteworthy for delays. "With Mangel's, Joseph E. Seagram, and all the others," Evan recalled, "we had a reputation for being smack on the ball every time." This was possible because Isaac Ross and Evan were, despite their entirely opposite personalities — perhaps *because* they were so different—an excellent working team. Ross's able organization and supervision combined with Evan's talents with such felicity that Ross Frankel, by 1938, was at the top of its field.

Meanwhile, Evan was more than ever the grand personage of the Frankel family, and hardly due alone to his business prosperity during an economically difficult decade. America was on the move again, in part, unfortunately, because the threat of war in Europe loomed larger every day. Many of Evan's brothers were working on their own private success stories, too. What continued to set Evan apart, especially after Abish Frankel died in 1935, was that he had fashioned for himself a life that was like a storybook American dream, complete with all the accessories. Irving's son, Ernest Frankel, now a Hollywood writer and producer, knew at the age of ten what mystique was when it walked into the room in the form of Uncle Evan:

"It was a real event when Uncle Evan arrived at a wedding or *bar mitzvah*. I knew that my father loved him and thought him wonderful and special, the brightest, quickest, smartest, and the most able, but that still didn't prepare us for Uncle Evan's visits. He would dominate his older brothers. I remember sitting on the floor and all the brothers and sisters were sitting around, and when Uncle Evan walked in, the whole focus of the room would change because he was now the center of it, and all would turn to him. Many of my uncles were tall and handsome, but Evan was the most. If you ever saw a family picture, it would be everybody, and Evan as the centerpoint!

"But what a life! That Packard convertible with twelve cylinders and a mile long, which some maharajah had turned down due to the expense, and Uncle Evan was driving it! And he spoke in a way I had never heard in my life except maybe in the movies. And he would do things like unaccountably reach into his pocket and give you a dollar. He was probably only making the equivalent of a very decent living today, but by

God we were convinced he was a multimillionaire. For me Evan was the earliest example I saw of someone who had become everything he wanted to be. It was his shining presence that made me believe that I might aspire to anything and everything."

Evan had this magical effect not only on his bright young relatives, but also on his many friends, particularly the female ones. If there were something that might be said to be merciful about the death of Evan's very religious father, it was that Abish Frankel was spared the age-old *tsores* of watching the development of his son's attraction to non-Jewish women. It was undoubtedly not an altogether easy adjustment for Evan himself. Evan had always respected his father's orthodox beliefs, but had rejected them for himself. When Abish died, Evan transferred his devoted regard to his sister Annie. She alone now represented the depth of commitment, the tradition, and the background Evan was so steeped in and that would not entirely free him.

Nevertheless, to take liberties with Ralph Waldo Emerson's verse: When Eros whispers low, Thou must, the Youth replies, I can. For all Evan's women friends were blonde, fair, and non-Jewish. More often than not, they were gorgeous models like Betty Williams, or from the world of the theater.

In 1937, an aspiring young Hollywood actress, Lucille Ball, was told by friends to call Evan Frankel when she came to New York. When she dialed his office, he promptly invited her out for a drink at the St. Regis. She replied that she was tired of the obligatory round of parties, restaurants, and bars and suggested she have that drink at his place. Evan was impressed already, even more so when they met at 5 Riverside Drive.

They took to one another in an amazing way and laughed a lot, a sure sign of the best of relationships. Since Miss Ball didn't have sufficient funds for the Barbizon Hotel for Women, Evan offered a highly attractive rate at 5 Riverside Drive, where she stayed for the balance of this trip, and several others in New York.

When, months later, Evan went to California on business for the Bulova Watch Company, the friendship ripened. Evan and Lucille went riding together at Arrowhead Springs and had their photograph taken in jodhpurs and riding jackets beneath the Joshua palms. They danced and barbecued and swam, and before long the friendship had turned to romance. Evan loved her inimitable brashness, and recognized her talent. Like all the young women who had preceded her, she found him captivating. Before the decade was out, Lucille Ball sent him a beautiful love note — of monumental proportion. It was, by any other name, a proposal of marriage.

Evan, with his candor, told Lucy that he was terrifically flattered, but that she was going places — without him. And, of course, he was right. They resumed their lives on separate coasts, remaining all these years exceptional friends and something of what they had been then, "an item."

Throughout the late 1930s, Evan's best friends remained the other musketeers, Emerson Thors and John Small, and their wives, Chou Chou and Amy. Evan was always a superb guest, having learned through his growing up how to be an "ex officio" member of another family. He loved the Thors and Small children. The Smalls had moved to White Plains, where Evan visited often to go riding with another good friend, Doug Warner. On summer weekends, everyone gathered at Doug

Warner's house in Ossining. There they swam at the lake and partied. With his prodigious side stroke, Evan ferried beakers of post-Prohibition gin between shore and raft and kept his friends from drowning, as they all sought some respite from thinking about the gathering war clouds in the international skies.

Above all, however, there were two new "loves" that entered into Evan's life during this period; within the next ten years he would have to choose between them. Although the loves were not people, but the towns of Woodstock and East Hampton, New York, it was to be a very difficult choice.

Woodstock, when John Small first introduced Evan to it, had been the site of an artists' compound for thirty years. Hervey White, an offbeat English utopian figure, had bought land there and laid out a compound for artists. In the winters of the 1930s, oil-burning potbellied stoves heated the individual shacks of artists who lived and worked there, often without paying rent. It was a time when there were many *luftmenschen*, people truly living on air. In this atmosphere of societal breakdown, Evan, who had some money, was like an ambassador from another world, able and willing to pick up the tab for those who had nothing. And he did it often and anonymously.

The Smalls introduced Evan to sculpture and to sculptors in Woodstock. John's sister Hannah was an accomplished sculptor and her husband Eugene Ludens a rising young painter. Through them, Evan met Raoul Hague, a sculptor who lived in Woodstock under unusually — even for that time — Spartan conditions. Dignified, talented, and poor, Hague's trademark was to serve Evan and his other guests Turkish coffee in a tiny but resplendently decorated cup. It was

77

all the elegance he could afford on his income of $5 a month.

The first art works Evan ever purchased were Hague's early Indian period sculptures in wood. The very first was a female with a long, sensuous, curving torso, which Evan installed at 5 Riverside Drive, and treasures it today. Since he always had a strong sense of line, and since his business involved woodworking and the design of spaces, it was natural for Evan to be drawn more to three-dimensional works than to painting. Sculpture allowed him to touch and to examine from every angle. Through his purchases, he lent valuable early support to Hague, Amy Small, and a number of other artists in Woodstock.

Chief among them, however, was the sculptor Harvey Fite and his wife Barbara, to whom Evan became very attached. An unusually strong artistic personality, Fite was a kind of "earthworks" artist thirty years before that term was coined. Although he was head of the art department at Bard College in nearby Annandale, New York, and taught conventional art and sculpture courses there, his legacy was to be a single monumental work on land he owned at Saugerties outside of Woodstock.

Fite worked alone on his property, acres of bluestone quarries out of which in the previous century had come the stone to pave the curbs and sidewalks of New York City. Using only old quarryman's tools, over a period of forty years he created what was to become known as Opus 40. Evan not only admired the obsessive tenacity of Harvey Fite's monumental stone construction, he was also moved by the way the artist transformed the landscape as he worked, creating a vast abstract geometric sculpture of stone and space, even more moving in its totality than in its individual parts. Further, Fite lived in the midst of it in a house of bluestone. None of this was lost on Evan when, in the 1950s, he took his property on Hither Lane in East Hampton and began — with tractor, tree, and sculpture — to transform that landscape into an enchanted opus of his own.

In 1938, however, Evan found and contemplated buying for himself some beautiful property in Woodstock adjacent to the Fites and in a swale of the Catskill Mountains. He gave serious thought to putting down roots in Woodstock, where he might stay weekends with friends or in the company of his nephew Seymour who, taking after Evan, had also found Woodstock very beautiful.

On other weekends, however, Emerson Thors led the merry company of Thors, Small, and Frankel out of New York City in another direction, due east on Long Island toward East Hampton, a resort town then some four hours from midtown.

In 1863, a boarder with military bearing named George McClellan came to the Mulford House in East Hampton to rest, after being relieved of his command of the Army of the Potomac. Perhaps people thought thereafter that East Hampton was a good place to come for refreshment of the soul or just to get away after a bad week at work. By the 1930s, East Hampton already had a fifty-year-old reputation as a gracious resort for rich and conservative New Yorkers. What really had put the town on the genteel vacationers' map, however, was the extension of the railroad in 1895, and the glamorous publicity given to the already beautiful town when the distinguished American artists Winslow Homer, Childe Hassam, and Thomas Moran settled there.

Emerson, John, and Evan were attracted by this tradition, even though by the 1930s that first generation of artists was already long gone, and the second World War had not yet brought the next, Europeans such as Marcel Duchamp and American modernists like Robert Motherwell.

In the company of the Thorses and the Smalls — practitioners and cognoscenti of art — Evan first descended on East Hampton. He stayed at the Sea Spray, Kozy Kabins, and other clean and modest inns and cottage compounds off the Montauk Highway. As Evan walked along East Hampton's Main Street, canopied by the leaves of centuries-old sycamores, as he took in the vast skies running down to the plane of the sea and the white of the dunes, he could easily agree with the Ladies Village Improvement Society that East Hampton was "America's Most Beautiful Town." He recognized that artists and people like himself would always be drawn there. So, although Woodstock continued to hold Evan through profound ties of his affection for the Fites and Smalls, Evan fell in love with East Hampton at first sight. Her brilliance had caught his eye, and although it would take more years to be consummated, the seduction had already begun.

V

On April 30, 1939, four short months before Hitler invaded Poland, triggering the second World War, the New York World's Fair opened. The 200,000 New Yorkers who arrived on opening day, having paid only a nickel to get to the fair by subway, found the seventy-five-cent general-admission charge exorbitant. Germany was conspicuously absent from the exhibits, since the fair's charming but outspoken president, Grover Aloysius Whalen, had called Germany "a museum of horrors." Hitler refused to respond to an invitation extended by such a man. Instead, he saved his millions for destruction.

Whalen was Evan Frankel's kind of guy. In addition to being president of the fair, Whalen was president of the Schenley Products Company. When Schenley, Seagram, and twenty other firms joined together to fund the building of the Distilled Spirits Exhibit, Evan brought back the business. The 1939 guidebook, "Building the World of Tomorrow," lists the credits for the Distilled Spirits Exhibit building as follows: architect, Morris Sanders; designers, Ross Frankel, Inc., and Morris Lapidus.

In a fair distinguished by the seven-hundred-foot Trylon, the two-hundred-foot-wide Perisphere, the General Motors' Futurama, and RCA's introduction of television, the Distilled Spirits building was outstanding and certainly one of the most notable achievements in Ross Frankel's fourteen years of operation. Situated on Rainbow Avenue in the "food zone," and within easy view of the heart of the fair, the Ross Frankel building beckoned with what was described as a fifty-foot-high "structural banner." The massive marquee declared simply, "Distillers," in block lettering beneath an Art Deco relief sculpture of grain stalks and other industry symbols. The facade was windowless, with extensive surfaces broken only by relief sculpture and a mural. In all this, the building conformed to the guidelines of the fair's Board of Design. By dictating its taste for Art Deco decor and advanced Bauhaus principles, the board put on display the work of America's premier young architects and industrial designers of the clean and uncluttered look.

As Evan became involved in this project, he could not but have been struck by the tremendous success of the Board of Design — and the prescience of Grover Whalen, Commissioner of Parks Robert Moses, and the other financial leaders of the fair's corporation. By allowing the architects and designers, not the business people and exhibitors, to have the last word on the look of the fair, they assured a low profile for their buildings, eliminated protruding signs, and used the city's magnificent skyline as a backdrop, creating an experience that grew with time in the memory of anyone who attended. Evan might well have remembered this experience, too, when years later, in the 1960s, as a member of the East Hampton Village Planning Board, he suggested the creation of an Architectural Board of Review. Its purpose: to resolve differences between developers' ideas and East Hampton's continuing visual traditions *before* the ideas became buildings.

From the point of view of design, the Ross Frankel/Lapidus team had probably reached its aesthetic apogee with its 1939 World's Fair building. Furthermore, Evan had succeeded, through the fair, in making Ross Frankel better known than ever before. He had enhanced its credentials, positioning the firm to do defense work should America be drawn into the European conflict.

In the fall of 1941, the war news from Europe made High Holiday services particularly somber for the Frankel clan as they gathered at the West Side Institutional Synagogue on 76th Street between Columbus and Amsterdam Avenues in Manhattan. At this holy time, accounts were reaching America from overseas that "Who shall live and who shall die" was not being determined by God this year but by the advancing German armies.

Still it was good to be together. Evan and most of his brothers had been long-time members of this orthodox synagogue, and Annie was now president of the synagogue and an influential counselor in the lives of all the Frankels. Jess Gross and his growing family, having overcome much hardship, were there for prayers every Saturday morning, and Seymour came often, too, as did Willie Ball.

Evan and Willie took special pleasure in watching Seymour's increasing independence. When a new bookkeeper at Ross Frankel quit, protesting that the job was too complicated, Evan encouraged Willie to teach Seymour how to keep the books. He learned quickly, and was soon keeping Evan's personal accounts. Eventually he took on the challenge of being part-time controller of his brother Jess's company. If a plea were needed to get into heaven, Willie told Evan, theirs would be that they helped Seymour to be self-supporting.

When war finally came, virtually the entire American economy shifted to defense. Ross Frankel set aside storefronts and began to prefabricate mess halls and barracks. Evan was given contracts to outfit transports, to fashion cases for shipping ordnance, as well as a dozen other projects where wood, creatively used, might be substituted for the metal products critical to the war effort.

Evan, charged with supervising these projects, was busier than ever, and his extensive network of personal connections grew. Emerson and John used to rib him about his name-dropping and joke that what was surprising was not who Evan knew, but who he didn't know. He was now on the road more than ever, traveling to the west coast, to Alaska, to Greenland. When he returned to his office at Ross Frankel, a letter from the Selective Service was waiting for him. At age forty, he was ordered to report to his draft board. The case was duly reviewed, and Evan was granted an exemption because he was doing essential war work.

Not long afterward, at a time of mounting concern about German U-boats prowling American coastal waters, Ross Frankel was awarded a contract to build wooden towers to house radar for an early warning system. The installations were to be built along the coast from Westhampton to Montauk. Evan and Isaac Ross were experts in wood. Now they had a chance to prove it to the War Department by constructing the towers entirely of wood, devising an ingenious way to build the frames on which the radar dishes sat. "The towers looked like elongated pyramids," Evan recalled, "with flat surfaces on top, and the machinery was in a room below the platform. There was a large tower at Main Beach, and several in Amagansett, but a German submarine approached in spite of them!"

The assignment brought Evan out to the South Fork of Long Island during the work week and for more extended periods than previous weekend jaunts. He had a chance to talk to the Polish farmers and to walk the land in Amagansett and Montauk, but above all in East Hampton. There he made his headquarters at the Sea Spray. In the spring he smelled the delicate scent of lilac, rising from the hedges farmers had planted to separate their potato fields and floating above the land like a perfumed haze. He might have seen an osprey soaring above with a fish in its talons. He recalled that an old salt told him that when the lilac fills the air in East Hampton, the weakfish run in the sea.

Much of what is important in Evan's life happened by the sea, and on September 7, 1942, someone was at Point Lookout, not far from Long Beach, waiting to walk into Evan Frankel's life. Athletic, glowing, twenty-year-old Peggy Goldsmith, standing there in her cute beach outfit, did not know she was waiting for Evan. She thought she was waiting only for the shuttle bus to take her to the Long Beach station. Then Evan and Seymour Gross came strolling by. The sun hung low in the western sky, and the cameras of memory clicked on, for what ensued was an old-fashioned — and very romantic — pick-up.

"I was brought up," Peggy remembered it, "never to take rides in strangers' cars, and I never had, but I think the fact that Seymour was there with Evan made it safe, and between Point Lookout and the Long Beach train station was maybe a ten-minute ride. It was a bright sunny day, so what could happen? Since it was shortly before my birthday, I decided to give myself a little present, and I accepted Evan's offer of a ride in his convertible Cadillac. As we were driving to Long Beach he discovered I lived in New York, and he drove me all the way there.

"That same night, he took me to a movie at Radio City Music Hall. I was still living with my parents, who were very strict, and I had to be home by eleven. In the middle of the movie I suddenly realized it was ten of eleven, and I just got up and left Evan and zipped home in a cab and got there just before my shoes turned to glass. I suspect that's one of the reasons Evan was interested. There's no aphrodisiac like innocence, and I was innocent as Cinderella."

Evan was drawn to this particular Cinderella. He was moved by the fact that she liked Seymour, and his nephew liked her. Peggy was a picture editor at Time-Life, near Rockefeller Center, and after work, in the months that followed, Evan often met her there at the rink. She was a terrific athlete and he delighted in watching her on the ice. Evan thought, Here I am a man of forty, a man of the world, and isn't Peggy as wholesome and wonderful as can be? Is it time, Evan pondered — as such mid-life meditations come to us all — to make her part of my future?

He still wasn't sure, but Peggy was. As they dated over the next two years, she fell head-over-the-proverbial-heels in love with Evan. They went to see *Oklahoma, Bloomer Girl,* and later *Carousel,* and every other musical in town. Evan was even beginning to invest small amounts of money in the theater. He was a Broadway angel, and Peggy was very impressed.

Evan took Peggy up to Woodstock with the Smalls and introduced her to the Fites and to Raoul Hague. He continued to collect Hague's sculptures and Fite's, and he bought five pieces of Amy Small's new work, too. The quintet of the Thorses, the Smalls, and Evan now became a regular group of six, with Peggy joining Evan for weekend travel and for anniversaries, birthdays, and other special occasions.

Sometimes all of them went out to East Hampton. Sometimes Evan and Peggy went alone. The radar tower work continued to occupy Evan along the South Fork, and he and Peggy would often ride up and down the coast, a surveyor's tripod sticking out of the back seat of the car. They stopped to read and sun themselves and then to swim, usually off the beach at Two Mile Hollow. Although she was the better athlete, in the sea Evan left Peggy — and just about everyone else — behind. He dived through the breakers, surfaced, and then dived again out to where the ocean was smooth. Then he swam along the coast for up to an hour before returning to the beach. There he talked to Peggy about his attraction to this place, about how one's whole outlook could be uplifted by the bracing astringency of ocean spray at land's end; of how he loved to walk or ride horses in the surf. Woodstock was mountainous and beautiful, Peggy heard him thinking aloud, but it was a long way from there to the sea.

"He really fell in love with East Hampton," Peggy remembered. "Way back then he was already calling it a 'living picture.' And I used to tease him about it as we drove. Any old scene that would come along on the road, I'd say, 'Oh Evan! Here comes another living picture!'"

The qualities that drew Evan to East Hampton had also drawn him to Peggy Goldsmith: simplicity, freshness, tranquility. But there was trouble ahead.

In the meantime, however, some new and ultimately determining elements had also entered Evan's life at Ross Frankel. While subcontracting work for the war effort continued to carry the firm nicely in the 1940s, as the post-Prohibition building boom had through the 1930s, Isaac Ross was no longer healthy. Evan and his partner continued in their genial if cantankerous relationship. Isaac would say, "I can't do this job for the price! You're killing me!" And Evan would reply, "You've done it before. You'll do it again." Both men knew that they had contributed equally to the success of the business. But Ross was fifteen years Evan's senior, and, even if he had not had to confront the onset of cancer, he would have been giving some thought to retiring. Evan, for entirely different reasons, was giving thought to the next phase of his life.

VI

The war was changing the world at large and everyone's smaller sphere as well. Morris Lapidus left the firm in 1943 to achieve the greater recognition that was not possible for him as an employee at Ross Frankel. Perhaps that was a sign of things to come. Edward Kimmel's arrival at Ross Frankel certainly signaled change, for the young attorney was passionately interested in real estate.

Evan and Isaac Ross had had some experience owning New York City property before. It was a natural adjunct to their business. As far back as 1934, in the depths of the Depression, the firm had acquired the mortgage on an apartment house in the Bronx, and over the years several other "hazards" were acquired as well. Evan explained: "Occasionally 'hazards' — places no one else knew what to do with — came to us because we were known. You didn't have to put much cash into a 'hazard' when you assumed the mortgage, and if you were a person or a firm with a solid reputation like us, you could get a mortgage without any trouble. So a few of these came right into our lap. But we weren't in that business and we treated them like investments, like stock, putting them into our pocket and not thinking about them afterward."

In the middle of the second World War, the real estate picture was similar. Buildings weren't full since men were off to war, and households had been combined; properties weren't generating enough rent to make them valuable. Landlords wanted to sell, and at sacrifice prices. In this environment, Ed

Kimmel induced Isaac Ross and Evan to buy the blockfront of property on Sixth Avenue between 53rd and 54th Streets. This was the first of a number of investments — all apartment houses in good solid areas — where prices, though now flat as a pancake, were certain to bounce back when the war ended. "So we stuck the deeds in the desk," Evan said, "and went about our business, and forgot about them!"

There was one property, however, that Evan did not forget about, indeed had not forgotten about since the first time he saw it in the 1930s. It was known as the McCord house, at 150 Hither Lane, East Hampton. Amy Small was with Evan the first time he set eyes on it:

"We were actually on our way only as far as Jones Beach that day; the Thorses and their kids, and Evan, and John and I and our kids. And then someone, I think it was Evan, said, 'Let's keep going.' It was impulsive, like Evan. It was only the third or fourth time we'd been to East Hampton. We drove on and got to the Sea Spray. But since we didn't have a thing with us, we went to the drugstore for toothbrushes and washcloths so we could stay over.

"The next morning, Evan went to get a shave and a newspaper. He always did that, especially in an unfamiliar place, so he could talk to the barber and find out what was really happening in a town. When he came back, he was flourishing the newspaper, and he said to us, 'I want to see this house. Who wants to go?'

"I went, and Emerson and John went, and we all thought Evan was truly crazy. The main house had burned down, and the carriage house was still being lived in, but was a real mess, with everything all overgrown. Evan fell in love with the place and the grounds, but the rest of us couldn't see it. Evan has an artist's imagination, and he was looking into the future then, beyond what was visible or easily apparent."

When Evan returned to the McCord house years later in 1943, he noticed that the carriage house had not been lived in for several years. There was a feeling of abandonment about it, with only a coal stove inside. The grounds were also more overgrown than ever. As he drove back to Manhattan, he must have been thinking that 150 Hither Lane was getting riper and riper for him.

It was not, however, only a question of buying a house. The larger question was whether, by this step, he was going to plant his flag in East Hampton as opposed to Woodstock. Beyond that, and perhaps the most important question of all, was whether he was going to be doing any of this with Peggy Goldsmith. After all, he had given her an engagement ring — or so she thought!

"Evan professed his love many times before the engagement ring," Peggy said. "Once he gave me the ring, he started to fall apart because of the family pressure. I never met Annie Gross, Seymour's mother, but apparently she thought I was some little gold digger, 'though she never met or knew me. That was rough. And my parents thought Evan was wonderful. I'm a quarter Jewish, if that's got any bearing, but my brother, a real bigot and anti-Jewish, was very upset, but had no influence as far as I was concerned. Mother and Father were delighted I had found someone I loved, and money had nothing to do with it. I couldn't prove to Annie that I loved Evan and would have without his money. There was no way to fight back. The fact that Annie brought him up, as a kind of mother, had a lot of influence on Evan. He told me she was going to go into mourning if the marriage proceeded. However, I often think it well may have not worked out. Evan is a maker of memories for many women. I think a woman always remembers her first love — and a man perhaps his last."

Despite honest efforts, sometimes well-intentioned communications with those we care for seem Delphic at best. Evan and Peggy went to see Paul Robeson's memorable performance in *Othello*. It may have given them some small consolation that the Moor and Desdemona were also having problems in their relationship, for a month after Evan had put the diamond ring on Peggy's finger, it was back in his pocket. She had returned it. Perhaps Peggy saw then — surely she did soon after —that she might also have misunderstood his gesture of giving her the ring. Couched as it was in a certain lightheartedness, she felt it might have actually been meant as an expression of continuing affection, not a pledge of commitment. Nevertheless, Peggy knew then something about Evan's complex character that all the women in his life and his many friends understood. They accepted the fact that you always had to have a sense of humor in dealing with him. However, they knew, too, that every joking or lighthearted gesture from Evan also carried within it a kernel of seriousness and truth.

Peggy and Evan remained good friends. She was his "steady" for years and got to know many members of the Frankel family. Evan's nephew, Frieda's son, David Plesser, insisted on calling her "Aunt Peggy" both to needle Evan good-humoredly, and to urge Peggy to fan the flames so Uncle Evan would marry her. But it did not happen. Evan recollected the affair in tranquility: "It was true that Annie strongly opposed my seeing non-Jewish women, but obviously I was a big boy! If I had found someone I wanted, it would not have deterred me."

What Evan came to realize through this love's labor lost

was that however much he admired the values of marriage and family, those institutions were personally not for him. His heart, talents, and boyhood experience had prepared him, not for a single profound attachment, but rather for a closeness to many people, kith and kin. This was precisely the life he was living and enjoying thoroughly. Although the term would still have been anachronistic in 1944, Evan was on the verge of being the master of an extended family of twenty-nine nieces, nephews, grandnieces, and grandnephews, and a multitude of interesting and devoted friends.

Moreover, he was drawing particularly close to certain of his young relatives in a relationship of intimacy and concern that would change, grow, and deepen over the years. Evan's god-child, Harrie Ellen Green, five years old in 1943, remembered her family's wartime trips up from Baltimore to visit Evan as if they had occurred yesterday. "There was such a flair about him, such an aura," she said. "There was for me then something almost pre-verbal, something in his nuance and manner, in the way he carried himself, and in his voice that set Evan apart. When he was in his tuxedo and evening cape, all dressed up for the theater, and he took my hand and walked with me to Rumpelmayer's for ice cream, I felt... elevated. Without question I was at that moment the greatest duchess who ever lived."

It was at this time also that Evan sent to his nephew Ernest, who was fighting overseas, a handsomely bound copy of Stephen Vincent Benét's *Burning City*. It was autographed by Benét, and below the autograph Evan wrote: " — Passed along to Ernest Frankel on his birthday — at a time when other cities are burning — with the hope that his next birthday will find these fires forever extinguished."

"That's how personal was Evan's devotion to his family,"

Ernest later said. "It wasn't money that touched us all. It was this singular kind of affection."

Luck came to Evan, and in some measure to everyone, with the end of the war. The Sixth Avenue property he had bought was sold for a sizable profit. With Ed Kimmel and his associate, George Jaffen, Evan had formed KFJ Ventures. Some of the other properties KFJ had accumulated during the war were also sold, so that in 1946, based on these several sales, Evan noted that, for the first time, he was no longer dependent on Ross Frankel for his income. More than that, he had completed one of the major rites of passage in his American Dream: Evan M. Frankel had become a millionaire.

"I remember when Evan got his first million," Peggy Goldsmith recollected. "We were at a dark bar, where we often met after work. We talked casually, but I knew something was up because he had that look in his eye. Then he produced a little black book, which he theatrically opened for me. It showed $1,000,000 from properties he'd sold. He was so proud that he was worth a million dollars!"

There were other signs that Evan's life was changing. Peggy was at 5 Riverside Drive one day to lunch with Evan. Not only was the cook, Pauline, bustling about, but her whole family had come in, to wash and iron, dust and clean. "He showed me these four people all running around for him," Peggy said, "and then Evan declaimed, 'Behold, my staff.'"

Evan told John Small that since he now had more money than any one man could need, he was ready to retire. John must have laughed, knowing his friend, because Evan could no more retire than could the ocean. Evan was only shifting gears and changing venues. The financial basis of a second career — and a kind of second life — had been laid.

As far as the world at large knew, however, Ross Frankel was still very much in business. Evan's sales letter to customers in September 1946 happily noted that wartime labor and material shortages were now a thing of the past, that Ross Frankel stood ready again to place "a designer-builder-manufacturer team" to work immediately, and that two decades of proven know-how would assure "an outstanding modern building at reasonable cost."

The letter even concluded that Ross Frankel facilities were expanding. Indeed, as the economy began to shift over to peacetime activities, Evan had hired Herman Neumann, a refugee German architect, whom he set to work on a group of new projects. There was a showroom for Emerson Radio on 21st Street, and also several complete buildings, from the ground up, in Birmingham, Alabama, and Dallas. But Evan asked his new employee to save some time, or, if he couldn't, to make some on the weekend, in order to drive out with him to East Hampton.

Depending on which account you read, Evan bought his Hither Lane home, the carriage house of the old McCord estate and the surrounding fifteen acres, for either $21,000 or $25,000. At either price, it was quite literally a fire-sale bargain, since the main house had burned to the ground in February 1920. *The East Hampton Star* reported the firemen were hampered by low water pressure and a long-standing problem in the alarm system. The column-two headline, next to the one describing the McCord house disaster, declared with unintended irony: "Firemen to Give a Public Dance."

Evan's purchase was part of a real-estate sales boom the likes of which East Hampton had not seen since the boom-crash cycle of the 1920s. Thirteen businesses had opened on Main Street and Newtown Lane in the first three months of 1946. Nine were operated by ex-servicemen, and all thirteen enterprises planned to operate on a twelve-month basis to accommodate the ever-increasing year-round population. Prosperity was clearly marching back to Long Island in the form of the returning American veteran. In the euphoria of victory, new problems, attendant on prosperity, were not yet in sight.

Evan, with Herman Neumann's help, set to work on the Hither Lane property. Since it was originally built as a carriage house, there were essentially two large open spaces, one downstairs and one up. The previous owner had installed a manually operated elevator between floors. It was a black wire cage with a hand crank to raise and lower it. Evan and Neumann designed and built a broad comfortable stairway to replace the primitive contraption. Under Evan's direction, Herman divided the upstairs space into master bedroom, bathroom, and guest bedrooms. The main space downstairs was relatively unchanged.

The house on Hither Lane thus underwent neither a gutting nor a restoration, but a limited remodeling, which became a touchstone for Evan's future work. His purpose was threefold: to create a modern, comfortable dwelling place out of what he found, to preserve intact as much as possible in the process, and to shift the aesthetic and visual emphasis from inside to outside. This latter aim was achieved by the installation of floor-to-ceiling windows the full length of the main room's west wall. These windows looked out upon grounds that were as yet untended and wild. Just beyond a small stone terrace, several large trees and tangled undergrowth were advancing on the residence like Birnam Wood to Dunsinane. In time, however, the new lord of this manor would deal with that as well.

When Evan wants something done, he sets his sights and it is done. He was so eager to have his own place in East Hampton that the time between the purchase of the house and the way it looks today was barely three months. "We worked in such a frenzied way," Herman Neumann recalled, "I disappeared from home just about every weekend. My wife was very unhappy!"

In 1946, in addition to Evan M. Frankel, East Hampton could boast of another remarkable new taxpayer. In the previous year Robert Motherwell had moved into his "industrial house" on Georgica Road, built for him by Pierre Chareau, one of Europe's leading modern architects. Although there were artists of note in East Hampton during the second World War, the arrival of a painter of Motherwell's stature accelerated the migration from New York City, bringing men like Jackson Pollock and Willem de Kooning who would go on to become the major American post-modernists. Between Frankel and Motherwell — and the changes they represented — East Hampton's post-war prosperity and artistic identity were ensured.

While the spacious shingled summer residences of East Hampton testified to the arrival of wealthy people in the past, there was something different about Evan and the particular wave he represented. For one thing, Evan was Jewish. Moreover, he had decided to pitch his tent on Hither Lane, south of the Montauk Highway and, in fact, cheek by jowl with the lands of the Maidstone Club. Since the Maidstone's establishment in 1891, the only Jewish people in sight may have been tailors and seamstresses serving the membership, described in the club's brochure as "men and women of good family and good breeding."

Although Evan was no stranger to non-Jewish preserves, and in fact had, in his fashion, sought them out to advance his business and social life, this was the first time he had bought property in such close proximity to such a place. He loved the land so much, he intended, from the beginning, to buy a great deal more. There was, however, a real problem, no matter how subtly or genteelly expressed, and Emerson Thors, who was with Evan when he bought the house, remembered a telling detail:

"The community was primarily Christian," he recalled, "and there may have been some ill feeling then that Evan, in buying the old McCord estate, was going to turn the place into Wantagh. So, in order to dissolve any unfriendliness, Evan put my name up along with his on the nameplate in front of the house, because I was already pretty well established in the community with the Maidstone people. After a short while, however, I asked Evan to take the nameplate with my name down, and he did. I don't want to cast aspersions on how the community was then and call it anti-Semitic. However, the truth is the truth."

A corollary to Evan's exceptional confidence that he can accomplish what he wants to accomplish was — and is — a healthy ability to ignore what can't be altered. So, since he wasn't interested in the Maidstone's golf course and as he had plans to build his own tennis court, Evan went his merry way, in public at least, even as his neighbors kept a watchful eye on his purchases and activities. After all, the exclusive club that did not accept Jews was a quite common phenomenon in the resorts and harbors of 1946 America. Nevertheless, in private, and to friends, Evan unburdened himself, damning religion's role in causing wars and exacerbating difference instead of helping to find all humanity's common ground.

Peggy, Evan's first female guest at Hither Lane, said she remembered Evan standing up at his bedroom window, from where, in 1947, he could see the steeply slanting roofs of the Maidstone Club in the distance. "Grow, trees, grow," he said aloud toward the group of pines he had just planted. "I wish you'd grow tall and fast so I wouldn't have to look out and see that place, that bastion of bigotry."

The circle of the Maidstone Club was only one of several different and expanding worlds within East Hampton, aptly called by Evan's friend and the *Star's* editor, Everett Rattray, a "cosmopolitan village." No shy wallflower and clearly no ordinary new citizen, Evan Frankel — investor and believer in the village — was getting to know everybody. In particular, he was getting to know its many artists.

One afternoon in September 1947, he was standing on his terrace with two of them, Ray Prohaska and Joe Wren. Wren, in addition to being an artist, was also a landscaper, and he was discussing with Evan the imminent overhauling of the grounds on Hither Lane. Ray Prohaska, however, wasn't contributing much to the discussion. Instead, he was pacing the terrace, and then the house, then outside onto the terrace again. Evan might have told him to relax a little, but Ray Prohaska couldn't; his wife was due to go into labor. The little girl she would give birth to would be named Elena, and twenty years from now she and Evan would meet and fall in love.

In 1948, the tercentenary of East Hampton, Evan bought another piece of land adjoining his own, and then, in one fell swoop, another one hundred twenty-five acres. By 1950, he had bought one hundred fifty more. What he said of these purchases was true of what was to come: "The price was very low, and it was easy to get a mortgage and not use a lot of cash. So I bought for fifty or two hundred per acre what is today worth $20,000 per acre! The point was, however, that I bought because the land was absolutely beautiful. I always looked for hilly land, here in a place where there is little, and I bought it most of all, because I loved it."

The East Hampton Star, whose reportage made a clear distinction between the activities of year-round residents and the comings and goings of the summer revelers, referred to Evan, quite accurately, as Evan M. Frankel of New York *and* East Hampton. For Evan, however, the balance was clearly shifting to the latter side of the conjunction. In his portfolio and, more importantly, his spirit, East Hampton gained precedence.

In 1949 Isaac Ross, ill with cancer, retired. Evan gave some thought to continuing the business himself. They had come a long way together since Paramount Contracting. As Ross Frankel Inc., they had truly been incorporated, functioning so well because the two men, so different, had yet been so complementary. Together, and with Morris Lapidus, they had done hundreds of stores, storefronts, offices, showrooms, and complete buildings. They had made a significant contribution to merchandising architecture. It would be tough to go on without Isaac Ross's hands. Moreover, the capital from the KFJ property sales had given Evan financial independence, and his continuing interest in the Broadway theater promised a new field to explore. In due time, therefore, the two old friends, with a simple handshake, liquidated the business. To underscore the amicability of the arrangement, Evan spent one of the Passover *seders* of 1949, even though the *seders* were nearly inviolable Frankel family occasions, at the table of Isaac Ross.

VII

The exits and entrances in people's lives are rarely as neat as those in a drama and usually require some kind of bridging. For some time, therefore, in expectation of the closing of Ross Frankel, Evan had been investing in Broadway theater. He was also involving himself with Guild Hall in East Hampton, and in particular with the productions of its John Drew Theater. It was a natural connection between his life in New York and his new community, where the John Drew Theater's first-rate summer productions reflected both the proximity of New York and the growing number of its theater people coming to perform, vacation, and settle along the South Fork.

Evan was primarily a backer of musicals. *Brigadoon* in 1947 and *Gentlemen Prefer Blondes*, with Carol Channing, in 1949 were among his successes. And he often brought in good friends, like Harry Green, to invest with him. When a production of *Brigadoon* came to the John Drew Theater, Evan decked out his house in plaids and dubbed the estate "Brigadoon," a name that has stuck. He played host to the cast, housing and entertaining them for the full run of the play at the John Drew. This was to be the first of numerous times Evan would offer the hospitality and shelter of his home to the casts performing at Guild Hall. Over the years, he helped support the poetry and museum programs there, contributed to seasonal exhibitions, and became a valued friend of the long-time director, Enez Whipple. Eventually, in 1981, he became a member of the Guild Hall board of trustees.

Evan was a Broadway angel all right, but an angel with a lot of deviltry in him as well. In 1950, as host to the cast of *Brigadoon*, Evan got to know Priscilla Gillette, an actress who had understudied for the co-star in the Broadway production. For years Priscilla's portrait hung in an honored place in the great hall of Brigadoon, East Hampton branch.

There was a particularly strong sense of theater combined with beautiful music in the Broadway production of Gian-Carlo Menotti's opera *The Medium*. When Evan, in the company of producer Walter Lowendahl, had seen it in 1946, they both felt that the production had been diminished by being on the same program with the Menotti curtain-raiser, *The Telephone*. Lowendahl suggested that Evan join him in producing a film version of *The Medium*, to be directed in Rome by the composer-librettist himself.

Evan was intrigued. He had not been to Rome since 1922, when he had been a penniless student, and he longed to return. However, even as Lowendahl consulted Evan in assembling the preliminary elements of the film, he delayed making a firm commitment. He still was not certain he wanted to go so suddenly from being a theatrical angel to being the co-producer of a film. But he was leaning.

It was characteristic of Evan to enter into a new endeavor with decisive, dramatic moves. Once he had chosen his course, he was not timid in implementing it. In real estate, he never purchased one or two acres. He bought fifty or a hundred. His entry into film-making was no different. He did it, typically, on a grand scale. It was to be a brief but star-studded stint, and the perfect investment of time, talent, and money. Evan had finally found an exciting new outlet for the strong theatrical strain that gave flamboyance to his character and style.

Herman Neumann, who continued to work with Evan on his East Hampton properties, used to marvel at the many roles Evan had played during the course of a single day's "performance" at Ross Frankel. No Willy Loman he! Evan was, in Herman's estimation, simply the greatest salesman who ever lived. "I was particularly impressed," he said, "by Evan's being able to speak to the president of a company about a very big job so well and so artfully, and then, after the meeting, we'd go to dinner and Evan would speak to the maitre d' in a totally different language, but just as naturally and just as well, and then outside to a cop on the corner in his argot! It was absolutely phenomenal."

In early 1949, Evan had met Sarah Churchill. The actress, daughter of the English prime minister, was already well launched on her career and had been signed to play the leading role in the touring production of *The Philadelphia Story*, written by Evan's East Hampton friend Philip Barry. She was in East Hampton being photographed by British photographer Anthony Beauchamp, who was also courting her.

Evan became friends with them both and in the same heady period also met another friend of Sarah Churchill's, a young singer named Margaret Truman. She had made her first concert appearance as a coloratura soprano in 1947, the first White House daughter to embark on a serious artistic career. In October 1949, Sarah Churchill and Beauchamp married, and in November she left to tour *The Philadelphia Story*. In the interim Evan had offered to assist her in the next stage of her career, her debut on the Broadway stage.

Soon afterward, however, early in 1950, Evan did finally accept the project to work with Lowendahl and Menotti on the film of *The Medium*. Marie Powers, Leo Colman, and Anna Marie Alberghetti were cast. The shooting went on from June to November in Rome, and Evan remembers the crew as being happy and close-knit. The conductor assisting Menotti was Thomas Schippers, and the American embassy people in Rome were on the scene, too, trying to do a little diplomatic basking in the glamour and good Italian-American relations the production was creating.

The sentimental star of the film was sixteen-year-old Anna Marie Alberghetti, whose English was a little shaky. Evan set himself up as her English coach for the film. Apart from this pleasant tutoring, his primary job was to see that the film came in as close to budget as possible. During breaks in shooting, Evan met Peter Ustinov, who was starring as the emperor in *Quo Vadis*, which was being filmed in an adjoining studio. The two men became friends and spent days off and weekends traveling up to Florence or Milan, often in the company of pretty Yugoslavian ingénues, imported to play extras in the Roman crowd scenes.

With the shooting of *The Medium* complete, editing in progress, and the New York première scheduled for the end of the year, Evan returned home. Having been away nearly six months, America seemed a somewhat strange place to the new producer, and with this new viewpoint he may well have seen it as a stage on which a national morality play was working itself out. For 1950 was the year "McCarthyism" was coined, "H Bomb" entered the language, and, in June, the Korean War erupted.

Evan resumed his friendship with Margaret Truman and Sarah Churchill, and they spent many a weekend at Brigadoon, which Sarah loved because it reminded her of her father's estate. As a nervous producer wondering what the reviewers would make of *The Medium*, Evan surely commiserated with Margaret Truman that season. Her father's letter to *Washington Post* music critic Paul Hume was the talk of the town: "I have just read your lousy review of Margaret's concert. . . . Some day I hope to meet you. When that happens, you'll need a new nose, a lot of beefsteak for black eyes, and perhaps a supporter for below."

Evan attended the première at the Sutton Place Theater with Sarah Churchill on one arm and Margaret Truman on the other. He needn't have worried about critics. *The Medium* opened in New York to rave notices. *Opera News* declared it "a remarkable, unique film that is not only pure opera but pure cinema . . . haunting, disturbing, moving — an historic film of depth and power." As the presenter of *The Medium*, Evan was tremendously proud of the film, which, over the years, became a classic.

Willie Ball, who continued to be Evan's accountant, said of him at this time, "If Frankel had ever told his father, an orthodox man from Europe, that some day he would entertain the daughter of the President of the United States and the daughter of the Prime Minister of Great Britain in his own home, his father would have said to him, 'You know, you talk like Joseph, who told his brethren that some day he was going to be so big they would look up to him and be beholden to him!' But Evan's father could not even imagine what America can open up to a man who has talent."

In the 1950–51 season, Evan poured most of his energy into John Cecil Holm's new play, *Gramercy Ghost*, starring Sarah Churchill. In supporting her career, Evan took a page from the book of his friend Kermit Bloomgarden, a successful independent producer, who said: "A producer is someone who throws out sparks that will stimulate author and director to make better use of their creativity; he's not a dictator." *Gramercy Ghost*, presented "in association with Evan M. Frankel," opened to good reviews at the Morosco Theater on April 26, 1951, with Brooks Atkinson of *The New York Times* writing, "Miss Churchill gives an adroit and mettlesome performance in a genuine comic style."

The play, however, was a mixed success financially. Evan was also a backer of *Billy Budd* that year, and went on to support the Broadway theater, particularly Kermit Bloomgarden's *Most Happy Fella* in the 1955–56 season and *Music Man* in the 1957–58 season. But after *Gramercy Ghost* he for all practical purposes voluntarily brought his career as a producer to a close. It was not merely that he had found it to be a high-risk endeavor and, although scintillating, not as businesslike as he had hoped. Beyond that, Evan had his own colorful life to produce, star in, and direct, and he was finding his days and nights in East Hampton more engaging than ever.

In his enthusiasm, he wanted his two best friends and their families to own places near him. He decided not to build the spectacular home Herman Neumann had designed for him in Woodstock. Instead, on property adjacent to Brigadoon Evan built two houses — the only two he ever built from the ground up in East Hampton — and he urged John Small and Emerson Thors to buy them. Evan made the terms very sweet, but he did not have control over the neighbors, specifically the Maidstone Club. And there, once again, lay the rub. John and Amy Small were sports people. In fact, Amy had come within a single putt of capturing the Connecticut Women's Golf Championship. Since they were Jewish, they would be barred from the Maidstone Club and its sports facilities. More importantly, the Smalls did not want their children growing up in a community that excluded them. The Smalls chose to remain in Woodstock.

Emerson, too, had the Maidstone Club on his mind. Some of the club's board members were friends, others were acquaintances from Wall Street, where Emerson was now a respected partner at Kuhn Loeb. "One of them called up back then," he remembered, "just after I'd sent my application in. He said, 'Em, I don't think you realize what sort of club we have.' I said, 'Why do you say that?' He said, 'Because you're a very good friend of Frankel.' I said, 'I'm an *extremely* good friend of Frankel's. Why?' He said, 'We have some questions about him and what he's doing and what he may do.' I said, 'Certainly if I do become a member of the club, I want to be assured now that he would be welcome any time I came to the club for dinner or lunch or whatever!' And this fellow said, 'No, he wouldn't be. He's Jewish.' And I said, 'In that case, cancel my application.'" Emerson Thors bought property elsewhere in East Hampton, but moved later to Water Mill, when his children were grown and there was too much grass to cut!

Evan was disappointed that his friends, who were as close to him as family, would not live nearby. However much he respected their decision, it was simply not Evan's way. Evan's way was to remain, and be himself. Evan's way was to turn anger into black humor. Evan's way was to enjoy the irony of watching everyone in town, Maidstone people included, increasingly eager to visit Brigadoon, there to meet the actors, musicians, authors, and politicians who sought Evan out. Celebrated men and women like Arthur Miller, Marilyn Monroe, Patrice Munsel, Senator Jacob Javits, Eli Wallach, and Ann

Jackson were, as the decade wore on, making Evan's home socially one of the most fascinating in East Hampton.

In 1952 Evan reached his fiftieth year in robust good health, maintained by riding, swimming, and moderation in food and drink. His standing in the theater world, and the mark he was making in East Hampton made the moment seem as if it were not the fiftieth year in his life, but the beginning of a whole new life. To mark the occasion, there was a party for him given by the Thorses, the Smalls, and Peggy Goldsmith. A superb picture editor, Peggy fashioned a birthday book for Evan, superimposing his face on photographs depicting events in his life: Here he was cleaning up on Wall Street, literally sweeping the street. Here he was pursuing his interest in finding Roman antiquities, as he appears to walk behind an ox in a Pompeian field apparently ploughing for archeological treasure. Peggy's album was extremely funny. Evan loved it because the mock-heroic humor showed both his achievements and his shortcomings, and it included both his origins and how far he'd traveled from the poor Carpathian hamlet of his birth. Simultaneously, it flattered and told the truth as only humor — and old friends — can.

A new friend entered Evan's life in 1952, in the person of Nora Bennett, cook and housekeeper. Playwright Bertolt Brecht wrote in a poem of the 1930s that Caesar may have crossed the Rubicon, but someone had to cook for him and the army. Nora cooked for Evan's army, and she deserves her own paragraph and far more, because for the next twenty years, until she died in 1973, friends and relatives stopping at Brigadoon found her modest but bustling presence inseparable from a visit with Evan himself. Her roast lamb or beef, the stews and puréed fresh vegetables, the vichyssoise and clam chowder, Yorkshire pudding and brownies were the simple and healthy fare Evan loved.

And not only Evan. *The New York Times* food critic Craig Claiborne, a frequent guest of Evan's and an admirer of Nora's talents, implored her for the chowder recipe. For years Nora, out of modesty, resisted. At last, Evan's close friend Joan Paley (now Cullman), prevailing on Nora's regard for posterity, was able to extract the chowder recipe slowly, as if a powerful runic formula were being reluctantly relinquished.

Joan: "How many potatoes?" Nora: "Oh, a few potatoes." Joan: "Ten?" Nora: "No, not so many." Joan: "Six?" Nora: "No, not that few!" Today Nora lives on through this hearty yet subtle dish, enshrined as "Nora's Fish Chowder" in Craig Claiborne's published cookbooks.

But Nora found her way to Evan's heart and those of his family and friends through routes even more profound than the alimentary. Joan Cullman again: "With Nora there, Evan didn't need marriage. She was hostess and mother, and very protective of Evan. She loved all of Evan's friends, and as many of us married, and came to visit with our kids, she would play with them, and read our fortunes in tea leaves. She was like our real grandma."

Having grown up in an Irish Catholic family of eighteen children in Galway, Ireland, Nora knew how to be with people. She appreciated Evan and his family of nine brothers and sisters, and particularly liked to meet the celebrities who came to Brigadoon. Yet there were sparks and disagreements between Nora and Evan, too, as in any close relationship. No less an authority on the subject than Nora's husband Charles said,

"They were like a married couple sometimes. Back and forth they would be flying at each other, not in a serious way, but he'd complain about something she'd bought or that she lingered too long talking at the post office. Then she'd toss a dish in the sink and say to Evan, 'In that case, I'm not cooking tonight!'"

John Bennett, Nora's son, who spent many an afternoon of his boyhood helping out at Brigadoon, now about fifty, had similarly noisy but affectionate memories: "Evan and my mother used to get into these big fights and actually would start calling each other ethnic names — in good humor: He'd call her an Irish biddy and then Mom would say, 'Sure and bigall, you're a crazy old kike!' Evan loved the sparring. They were very close for a long time, and all the hassling and spats were really enjoyable to them. It was all based on fondness."

Around the same time that Evan retained Nora as part of *his* long-range plan for the future at Brigadoon, the village of East Hampton decided that it needed a master plan. While development was occurring, it was by no means threatening. Yet in September 1952 the village fathers discovered to their dismay that there wasn't even an up-to-date and official map of the village. On the nineteenth of September, therefore, the Village Board enacted an ordinance creating a Planning Board. Once they secured a map, the Planning Board's mandate would be to create a master plan providing for future development of East Hampton. "All villages are not like Levittown," declared the Village Board's lawyer in explaining the need for the Planning Board. "This Planning Board," he said, with prescience that would resonate in the battles of the years to come, "is not magic. It is a tool, and like every tool, it is only as skillful as the hand that made it." The ordinance called for a Planning Board to comprise five people, two Village Board members and three other citizens of the village. Evan M. Frankel was one of those citizens appointed to the first Planning Board.

It was in a way a remarkable appointment, for Evan was still a relative outsider to East Hampton. He was still referred to in the press that announced his property purchases as "Evan Frankel of New York and East Hampton, backer of New York stage successes and real estate developer." Perhaps the Village Board expected Evan to turn into a major developer of land in East Hampton. In all likelihood the Board didn't know what Evan was really up to and was desirous early on of having him become a team player.

His role on the Planning Board, however, was to be anything but that. In little more than a decade, through both good luck and farsighted vision, Evan would be in a position to hold onto and preserve, with little or no development, large amounts of the most beautiful land in East Hampton. Moreover, he would increasingly be a gadfly buzzing at the ear of fellow Planning Board members, and especially newly arrived builders who threatened to develop too quickly or too shabbily.

But this was still to come, for the cantankerous times in East Hampton did not arrive until the 1960s, and Evan's early tenure on the Planning Board was, like life in the village of East Hampton, amicable, sedate, and sometimes even sleepy.

Abish and Nettie Frankel, 1906.

"Kid Dictionary," Evan at age twelve, from an old print.

With three friends in Rome, 1922. Evan
is second from right.

The Frankel boys: *(back row, left to right)* Phil, Irving,
Mayer, Dave, *(front row)* Aaron, father Abish, Evan.

"Imagine! I was riding a horse. I was a gentleman!" At Briarcliff Lodge, Westchester County, New York.

The "mile-long" right-hand-drive Packard, with Emerson and Chou Chou Thors in the rumble seat.

On the beach with friends on Long Island.

In Bermuda with Emerson, and with model Betty Williams.

The young president of Ross Frankel Incorporated.

In Bermuda for business and pleasure.

CREATORS OF
DISTINCTIVE
INTERIORS
○
UNUSUAL
FRONTS
○
TELEPHONE
LONGACRE 5-3885

ROSS · FRANKEL
INCORPORATED
OPERATING NATIONALLY
402 WEST 27TH ST. NEW YORK I, N.Y.

September 9, 1946

Gentlemen:

At war's end, when labor and material shortages became even more pressing, Ross Frankel Inc. decided not to accept all the jobs offered, but to continue to turn out fine work reasonably and on schedule.

Today, a year later, we have a record of completed projects which show that beauty, precision and economy are best served when the talents of designer, builder and craftsman are pooled. Our designers and draftsmen prepare plans; our field superintendents direct erection of the structure; skilled craftsmen in our factory build fixtures. That is why we produce on time and complete contracts with the attention to detail which characterizes Ross Frankel construction.

These are facts. We produce at fair expenditure because we have the hard-earned "know how" to help lick material and labor shortages. We have the designer-builder-manufacturer team, a technique developed in the past two decades, which continues to prove successful.

Plans for enlarging our production facilities are progressing. We hope we may soon put these facilities at your disposal; and, that you will allow us to study your designing and construction problems and prepare recommendations assuring you of an outstanding modern building at a sensible cost.

We trust we shall have the pleasure of working with you when our plans materialize.

Very truly yours,

ROSS FRANKEL INC.

Evan M. Frankel
President

Ross Frankel's 1946 sales letter.

On the following pages: the promotional brochure.

Corner view of office, Bulova Watch Company. Concealed lighting, walnut panelling and decorative map make for dignified elegance.

Interior of Mangel's Atlanta, Ga., store. Hosiery and lingerie departments designed to fit their special needs. The jewelry department in center of floor contains concealed stock.

ROSS FRA

OPERATES NATIONALLY,

THE STO

Bags require dramatic setting and special lighting to afford maximum sales appeal. Cases allow for extensive displays.

This cash and wrap desk of Mangel's Atlanta, Ga., store is centrally located, commanding a clear view. The desk is of attractive design and sturdy construction.

Showroom for Manhattan Undergarment Co. Cove lighting and glass partitions produce an elegant effect. The curved wall conceals a sales booth, as do the glass bricks, an undesirable view.

The Distilled Spirits Industry Exhibit building with its fifty-foot marquee, 1939 World's Fair.

With Bill Cleland *(on Evan's left)* president of the
Joseph E. Seagram Company.

Atop the all-wood radar platform for coastal defense at the beach in Montauk.

Romancing Lucille Ball at the Arrowhead Springs Hotel.

At the Stork Club with Peggy Goldsmith, 1944. *Below:*
picnicking with Amy Small and Doug Warner *(to Evan's
right)*, and posing with Emerson Thors and John Small.

op: The ten Frankel siblings:
(standing, left to right) Irving,
*h*il, Claire, Aaron, Dave, Yetta,
*v*an, Mayer; *(seated)* Frieda and
*n*nie. *Right:* reciting the *Kiddush*
the sacrosanct family *seder,* with
ster Annie and her youngest son,
*a*ron Gross.

Evan and other guests at the wedding of Ernest and Louise
Frankel, October 1944.

In East Hampton with *(left to right)* John and Amy Small and
Chou Chou Thors. *Below:* With the Smalls and their daughter
Judy.

In Woodstock: *(left to right)* John Small, Emerson Thors, Herman Neumann, Evan flanked by the sons of John and Emerson, and Harvey Fite.

Lighting a cigarette for
Fite at one of his quarries.

Seymour Gross and friend.

Evan's fiftieth birthday party: *(left to right)* Emerson, Evan, Walter Lowendahl, Peggy Goldsmith, *(in back)* Amy Small.

Below: Toasting friendship and the next fifty years; Patrice Munsel is beneath Evan's raised glass.

VIII

On June 2, 1953, in Westminster Abbey, three days after Edmond Hillary and Tenzig Norgay had reached the summit of Mount Everest, the Archbishop of Canterbury crowned Elizabeth Queen of England. While most Americans watched the coronation on the television sets that had become standard in the corner of the living room, Evan took in the pomp and circumstance in person as an honored American guest, in the company of his friend Sarah Churchill. After the ceremony, there were a number of receptions, one given by Winston Churchill at Blenheim Palace. There, the various legations moved down the official receiving line in which Evan stood, as escort to Winston Churchill's daughter. When the American contingent approached him, Evan heard, "Evan Frankel! You're the last person I expected to see. What are *you* doing here?" It was the voice of one of the official American representatives, whom Evan knew slightly from New York. She was so astonished to see Evan on the receiving line shoulder to shoulder with Winston Churchill and British royalty that her surprised exclamation filled the hall.

The moment might have embarrassed a more inhibited person, but Evan loved it. He knew precisely why he was there. Just as Mount Everest was a peak Hillary had to scale, this occasion was a kind of social pinnacle for Evan. It was not only that he was Sarah's friend and had been asked to fill in for husband Anthony Beauchamp, whom Winston Churchill detested. Evan felt that in a way he belonged here. Prior to the coronation he had attended receptions at various English country estates. He'd also gone to Oxford and Cambridge, a digression that reminded him of the near decision of twenty years before to enter Magdalen College. Evan felt so utterly at home in Sarah Churchill's company and on the grounds of the estates he had visited — and indeed in all styles English — that the whole experience inspired him.

After his return to New York, Evan was more mindful than ever of the need to preserve land in its natural beauty, and his passion for Nature was renewed and enriched. He was certain that America, forever building itself anew, destroying and building in a sometimes aimless, often ugly cycle, could use this sense of the heritage of the land. Was he himself not European? And what was, essentially, the difference between peasant and king, if not land? And why should Evan not provide an example on his estate in East Hampton and on the property he was accumulating?

Ownership of primarily vertical property in Manhattan, he reflected, had simply not provided him with the sense of purpose that the beautiful lands of the South Fork now gave him. The coronation of Elizabeth, therefore, was not only a heightened social occasion for Evan, but an aesthetic-spiritual watershed as well, augmenting and refining his own long-held ideas about the land. In ways tangible yet immeasurable, it guided hereafter both Evan's personal style and his choice of clothes, the look of his house and grounds, and perhaps, most importantly, his evolving policy of keeping his holdings in farmland and woodland as untouched as possible by the builder's hammer.

After attending the coronation, Evan went to Rome, where he met a business friend, Joe Weinstein, and his wife

Bobbi. Bobbi, who had never met Evan before, remembered that first meeting and Evan's remarks: "We met him as we were both walking through the swinging door into the lobby of this wonderful hotel, and my husband asked Evan where he was staying, and he answered, 'At the Flora, the poor man's hotel.'" The Flora was a swanky place indeed, and Evan's remark was a typically ironic Frankelism, with exaggerated understatement.

This meeting was the beginning of yet another lifelong close friendship. Evan invited the Weinsteins to Brigadoon for Labor Day brunch that year and showed them East Hampton. Soon they were renting in East Hampton for the summers, and eventually they bought their own place. The Weinsteins were among the first of scores of people Evan would enthusiastically introduce to East Hampton and in whom he would inspire a special regard for the scrub pines, the dunes, beaches, marshes, bogs, bays, inlets, and shore that he loved.

When he returned to America, Evan discovered that not just he, but the whole country, was being swept by a post-coronation Anglomania. One of its effects was to elevate Sarah Churchill's theatrical star even higher. Evan delighted in her success as host of the nationally televised Hallmark Hall of Fame, and in her presentation of *Hamlet*, in which she played Ophelia. He squired Sarah and Anthony Beauchamp about New York, and they continued to be regular guests in East Hampton.

Evan's nephew David Plesser remembered a 1954 beauty contest he sponsored. Sarah, at Evan's request, had agreed to be the chief judge. "Our stores, Plesser Appliances, were running a big beauty contest, a kind of promotion at the Rivoli Theater in Hempstead," he recalled. "Since Sarah Churchill had given Evan a commitment to be the judge, I'd gotten *Newsday* to cover it. But here it was seven, then eight o'clock. The photographers were there. The contest was under way. And no Sarah Churchill.

"What had happened was that, without much warning, Sarah's father Winston Churchill had come to New York the night of the contest, and she suddenly had to attend a dinner for him at Bernard Baruch's house in the city. By nine o'clock, I was about to give up, when I heard sirens and alarms, and I ran out front of the theater to see Sarah Churchill, Anthony Beauchamp, and Evan arriving, complete with a police escort. They had gone through every red light on the road, the police leading the way. Evan had dragged Sarah away from Bernard Baruch and Winston Churchill to get to the Plesser Appliance Stores beauty contest! Family makes deep obligation in Evan."

With visions of England still fresh, Evan, with his usual alacrity, now acted on his insights and intuitions. First, he eased out of the house remodeling activity that had engaged him and Herman Neumann since Evan's purchase of his own house in 1946. This had never been a business per se. Evan had merely acquired property — usually houses, old and charming but not dilapidated, and almost always beautifully set among trees — without having a fixed idea of what to do with them. He had refurbished the houses and sold them as needed to generate income in order to acquire his farmland, woodland, and oceanfront property. This activity, as Herman Neumann remembered it, was an inimitable Evan potpourri: "On weekends Evan would show people what he was doing at his own house and others. It was all partly business, partly social, partly pleasure, a very unusual mixture."

With the changing economy, however, and the aggravation that came with remodeling houses, this work grew tiresome for Evan. But since he needed some income, he decided to purchase, seriatim, in the early-to-mid-1950s, three adjacent commercial properties on Newtown Lane, near East Hampton's main intersection: Odd Fellows Hall, an old garage, and the building known as the old post office. The 1897 Odd Fellows Hall, which had genuine architectural distinction, as well as the garage and the abandoned post office, had been allowed, in Evan's phrase "to go to wrack and ruin." He proceeded, in accordance with his aesthetic principles, to preserve and enhance their original charm and integrity even as he modernized the property for appropriate commercial use.

"Appropriate commercial use" for Evan meant a use that was in the spirit of the community, and more often than not it was that criterion that guided him in his choice of tenants for these refurbished spaces. The former post office, therefore, was launched as a revival movie house. Later it became the home of an independent theater company. Other occupants included interesting but not always profitable artistic ventures that Evan, to some extent, quietly subsidized. He leased them space primarily because he felt the village would benefit by having them around. The Odd Fellows Hall was a school for a while, and in years to come it would house the Upstairs Gallery, a gallery and arts center operated by Ray Prohaska's grown daughter, Elena.

For the twenty years that Evan held these properties, he treated them as a kind of private stewardship that artistically enriched East Hampton. He also succeeded in keeping an architecturally important stretch of Newtown Lane intact and safe from design changes he felt would not be right for East Hampton. If, as people joked, one of the worst sins you could

141

commit in East Hampton was to render something ugly or tacky, Evan Frankel was, by that measure, one of the village's most virtuous citizens, and staunchest defenders.

By 1955 Ross Frankel had already been a memory for five years, and the Great White Way, Evan had decided, just might survive without him. Yet someone who is essentially a producer, like Evan, must have a project to engage him, or he gets cranky from the bottling up of his creativity. Evan, therefore, began with Ed Kimmel another KFJ venture. Executive House, an apartment building they erected at 225 East 46th Street in Manhattan, was destined to be their last and most interesting project.

Well before May 1955, when the Third Avenue El ceased service and was demolished to make way for apartments and offices, midtown New York had been the scene of rapid high-rise development. Yet, as Evan might have seen on a clear day from his penthouse at 5 Riverside Drive, most construction had stopped at Third Avenue. Beyond was a tenement and smokestack zone. It was in that area that Evan and Kimmel placed their building, for they guessed that an area with Grand Central to the west and the United Nations to the east must eventually rise in desirability and value. That guess was similar to Evan's guess in 1946 that property at land's end and only a hundred miles from midtown could also only go up. In hindsight, it all seems obvious. In fact, the ability to perceive the obvious, more accurately described as farsightedness, plus a little good luck, is what makes millionaires.

And indeed when Executive House was finished, in May 1956, and began renting, it turned out to be one of the most successful apartment houses in New York. Evan had broken new ground, not only with the location of the building, which eventually pointed the way to the transformation of a slum, but also, and most significantly, with the design and innovative use of the lobby space, which the building's architect had left entirely in Evan's hands.

The lobby of Executive House was, in Evan's phrase, "dedicated as a gallery." It was possibly the first building whose public space was used for the exhibition of contemporary art. And not just any art, but changing monthly exhibitions of the best of the new modernists. Many of the artists who displayed their work at Executive House were East Hampton neighbors either of Evan's or of his friend, the artist Alfonso Ossorio. Evan had asked Ossorio to take charge of scheduling the exhibitions, and take charge he did. The paintings and prints of Pollock and de Kooning, the burnished metal sculpture of David Smith (Evan preferred sculpture), and the work of dozens of other artists were put on view. The exhibitions generated tremendous interest and positive publicity, setting a precedent for the use of modern art in lobbies, plazas, and other open quasi-public space throughout the city.

Works of art were sold, and apartments were rented to interesting people. Everyone, particularly Evan, was happy. He was dressed in a very English style now, often in a slightly worn Norfolk jacket with ascot, and he kept a comfortable art-filled apartment. His ground-floor headquarters in Executive House was more like a living room than an office. From here he phoned his friends, like Joan Paley (Cullman). "Sweetie," he said to her, "stop by Executive House after work, and I'll rent you an apartment. And if I can't rent you an apartment, I'll still take you to dinner."

It was a giddy and particularly successful time for Evan, and he was entranced with Joan, too. She worked for Evan's good friend Frank Farrell, a columnist for *The World Telegram and Sun*. Frank's beat was the business-social scene, and he gave Evan, and particularly Executive House at this time, considerable publicity, referring to Evan regularly in his column, always as "architect-realtor Evan M. Frankel."

More important to Evan was Frank's introducing him to the bright, vivacious, beautiful Joan. They went to the theater and to museums or just walked together through Manhattan. "Evan would talk about a town house," Joan remembered, "or we would linger in front of sculpture in a window, or we sat at the reflecting pool in the Metropolitan Museum. Evan always picked out a column or an architectural feature of a space and talked about it in a way that opened my eyes and heightened the experience. There were so many of these simple pleasures with him." Joan was destined to occupy a remarkable succession of roles in Evan's life — affectionate companion, devoted helper, and confidante — and to become one of Evan's most treasured and loyal friends.

Frank Farrell and Evan had a lot in common, and particularly a congenital inability to separate business from pleasure. Along with Sarah Churchill and Tony Beauchamp, Frank became a kind of weekend fixture at Evan's house in East Hampton during the 1950s and 1960s. Evan dubbed him his "grand seneschal," the dispenser not only of libations but of hearty infectious laughter that boomed the length and breadth of summer afternoons at Brigadoon.

Evan's generosity to family never flagged. When his nephew Ernest's first novel, *Band of Brothers*, was published, Evan simply took over publicity and promotion. He hired a secretary to get out direct mail and handle phone calls from his Executive House office. He hired a publicity firm and conferred with the editor-in-chief and the marketing staff. He demanded and received "plugs" from Frank Farrell, Dorothy Kilgallen, Ed Sullivan, and many others. He arranged radio and TV interviews, trumpeted the critical applause, and read reviews to anyone who would listen — and made a friend and ally of everyone he met!

As a sort of sabbatical from work on Executive House, Evan decided to put in a pool for himself on Hither Lane. Or rather, he *produced* his poool, orchestrating and conducting its construction. From a director's chair on the lawn overlooking the site, he made certain that the finished creation would resemble a Pompeian bath he remembered from his travels. The raw material was the charred brick ruin that was the foundation and basement of the original house. Evan excavated the debris of twenty-five years, and landscaped an open end, with a stream cascading over boulders into the pool. For humor he retained the fireplace complete with logs and andirons. It was now in the wall facing the center of the pool at water level as if it stood ready to warm the bathers. Evan installed underground lights — probably a first even for East Hampton — and surrounded the whole with cannas, portulacas, and other flowers of wild beauty. When the first guests arrived with their swimsuits, Evan remembered the way Woodstock artists swam in Harvey Fite's quarry. "A pool is not a laundromat!" he benignly hectored his friends. "Off with your clothes!"

Fame — and gossip — about Evan's pool, which he called his "ruin," spread throughout East Hampton and beyond. *The New Yorker's* "Talk of the Town" reported, in August 1957, that "Mr. Frankel's Folly" was indeed a delight and qualified as a folly since it fulfilled the definition: "a structure erected for whimsical ornament on a gentleman's estate." It was, indeed, the first enchanted installment in the making of Evan's personal kingdom of fountains, trees, sculpture, fanciful constructions, and labyrinthine landscape. East Hampton had never seen the likes of it before.

Not only for private contemplation and frolic, the grounds and "the ruin" were for the neighbors to enjoy as well. Evan was delighted to have them come over, particularly if they had kids. Raymond Bigar, a long-time neighbor, remembered: "One day by his pool, Evan was telling my daughter, Dominique, then age five, that he had been to a party the previous night, and although there were lots of beautiful girls at that party, there were none as beautiful as she was. Dominique walked back to our house with my wife, who said to her, 'Darling, you can't listen to everything Evan tells you because, you know Evan, he tells this to everybody.' And Dominique said to her, 'Yes, I know that, Mother, but it's so pleasant to listen to him.' Dominique and all small children adored Evan. He would have been the greatest grandfather there has ever been!"

Evan was fifty-five years old and cutting a swath through East Hampton, both as the grandfatherly, but flamboyant, master of his manor, and as the owner and protector of increasingly sizable acreage. A complex, ironic man, eager to live life to the fullest, can sometimes be puzzling or unsettling to his neighbors. However, Evan insisted that his desires were simple. What he articulated to *The New Yorker,* he told *Newsday, The New York Times,* and the dozen other publications that covered his activities in the decade to come: "In recent years I've become concerned about the tide running against beauty in this country — billboards along the roads, houses crowded together on tiny development plots, and so on. Since I came out here, I've been trying to do something about it by buying up tracts of beautiful, unspoiled land in and around East Hampton. Not for resale, but simply to be looked at in their natural state."

The more East Hampton pleased Evan, the more days he added to the weekend. In the city, where he still spent considerable time, he was troubled by the noise, the overcrowding, the pollution, and the ugliness of the office towers rising higher than ever over midtown. By all accounts of his friends, Evan's eyes were open earlier than most to how the sky was disappearing from the skyline and to how Madison Avenue's few trees seemed never to get enough sunlight.

A friend in the real estate business told Evan that the Federation of Jewish Philanthropies was desperately in need of land to build a new headquarters. Evan had bought a property on 57th Street with a parcel of land attached, and his colleague asked him for it on behalf of the Jewish organization. "Why not?" Evan said, recalling the occasion. "I was doing very well. And I have always been a good Jew! So I gave it." Apart from its generosity, this gesture was one of leave-taking as well, because Evan was tiring of the city and was preparing to forego it altogether.

Among New York City's treasures that he would miss most was Steinberg's Dairy Restaurant, then at 82nd and Broadway. Eating there one afternoon in 1958 with his friend Jeffrey Potter of Manhattan and Amagansett, Evan was considering what he would do with a funeral parlor property he'd closed on the previous day. A writer, riding companion, and business partner of Evan's, Potter had helped Evan with the excavation of his pool. Now they met twice a week for business lunches at

Steinberg's, where Evan was an honored regular. He particularly delighted in introducing his non-Jewish friends to the world of farfels, kugels, and old-fashioned Jewish waiters eager to make sure you got enough to eat. Evan was something of a hero to the waiters there, perhaps because of his ebullient style, perhaps because he was related to the owners, his brother Mayer's in-laws.

"After we left Steinberg's," Jeffrey Potter said, "Evan, very elegantly dressed as usual, took me on a tour of his recently acquired building in the Lincoln Center area. It was small and had been the site of a funeral home. As we walked through, he told me his plans for it. When he reached the back room, he opened the door, and we found that whoever had vacated the property had left a little something behind! Laid out on a table was an elderly cadaver! I looked at it and Evan looked at it with some horror and then he said, 'My God, and it's even got a hole in its sock!' And, sure enough, a big toe was sticking through the sock. So, we made a hasty retreat and Evan went off to find out who had left that body behind on his property."

Perhaps the cadaver was an omen for Evan that he should put his New York City real estate activities to rest. In any case, he had been planning on doing precisely that. He resold the funeral parlor property, and settled his seemingly irreconcilable arguments with Edward Kimmel by relinquishing his share of Executive House in exchange for Kimmel's share of the partnership properties in East Hampton. This business parting, unlike the one with Isaac Ross, was not very pleasant. But Evan was happy enough with the chief result. It was 1960, and he now owned no property in New York City, although he continued to rent the 5 Riverside Drive apartment. He now belonged to East Hampton, just as some six hundred acres of East Hampton now belonged exclusively to him!

During these years Evan became, by all reports, East Hampton's unofficial ambassador in New York City. One New Yorker would mention East Hampton to another, and frequently Evan's name would come up in the conversation because Evan had such an extensive network of friends and acquaintances. As a result, dozens of people coming to East Hampton for the first time would end up at Hither Lane, where Evan, his delight in meeting new people keen as ever, would greet them at the door, show them his home, grounds, and sculpture. Then he would grab a supply of Nora's brownies for the road and pile the visitors into his Jeep to give them an unforgettable tour of East Hampton's "Courbet"s, and "Van Gogh"s, all of the scenic delights he called its "living paintings."

Evan Frankel was also a beacon for many well-to-do Jewish people, new arrivals in East Hampton, who had attained financial and social status only after the second World War. Often following Evan's advice and example, they carefully improved the beautiful properties they bought. If any old-time East Hampton families still harbored negative stereotypes about Jews, the evidence was increasingly ample — in the love, concern, and respect being shown to land and village — that these prejudices were unjustified. Evan, simply by living the life he chose to live, without raising his voice (too much!) or his banner (too often!) was in his own way a social pioneer, making an enormous contribution to East Hampton.

*   *   *

He was, therefore, not surprised but delighted and intrigued in 1959 when the small year-round Jewish community in East Hampton asked him to help them build a temple.

The year-round Jewish residents in East Hampton were unlike those of most towns in America, where a small Jewish community tends to be cohesive. The Jews living year-round on the South Fork were a diverse lot, coming from many different places and Jewish backgrounds. The proximity of the city, where they, like Evan, had family and prior temple affiliations, the cosmopolitanism and resort quality of village life, and the presence of a higher than average number of intermarried couples had made a temple of their own seem unnecessary to the Jews of East Hampton. For years they had driven the eight miles north to Sag Harbor's Temple Adas Israel for sabbath and holiday celebrations.

However, with increasing Jewish populations in the towns from Southampton to Montauk, and with their children nearing *bar* and *bas mitzvah* age, they believed it was time to do what communities of faith have always done to perpetuate themselves. They decided to put down institutional roots. Therefore, in July 1959 the Zeldins, Markowitzes, and a handful of other founding families incorporated as the Jewish Center of the Hamptons. They elicited pledges from their members — twelve families at most — and took an option on a one-acre property just outside of town on the Montauk Highway. They commissioned an architect's plans for a temple building. These they presented to Evan Frankel.

Bernard Zeldin, the president of the proposed Jewish Center, and Irving Markowitz, its treasurer, had picked their man well. Evan had never concealed his Jewishness since his 1946 arrival in East Hampton. Since then, spending increasingly more time in the village, both as private citizen and as Planning Board member, Evan was easily the most visible of well-to-do Jewish East Hamptonites. Although he took no part in the specific activities of the year-round families, Evan had counted himself spiritually as one of them. Indeed, the principle of Jewish community was in Evan's blood. So he supported the proposal and, although for the time being he did not make a specific commitment of funds, he gave Bernard Zeldin and Irving Markowitz a list of other people to call on, including the philanthropist Jacob M. Kaplan. Evan then asked the community leaders to report back to him the response they received to their proposal.

Meanwhile, he studied the architect's rendering. Evan was sufficiently steeped in Jewish tradition to understand that, since the destruction of the temple in Jerusalem, it had never been simply a building that had kept Jews together over the millennia. It was also a book, a sabbath, and any ten men gathered anywhere, in the humblest surroundings, even under a tree. It was not *where* you prayed but *if* and *how* you prayed that counted. Nevertheless, Evan knew more than most about humble surroundings. Moreover, he had spent many years of his working life dueling with architects and designers, and in matters of taste he accepted nobody's authority but his own. As positive as Evan was about the idea of a Jewish temple in town, he found the plans for the suggested building unattractive and unsuitable.

But, *mirabile dictu*, Evan happened to own the former Borden estate, a large imposing shingled house built at the turn of the century at 44 Woods Lane. The residence, Evan thought to himself, had sufficient space and grounds to make a wonderful temple. One story has it that during this interval, while Bernard Zeldin and Irving Markowitz were prospecting for other support for the temple, Evan took an informal survey of his own to find out what some of his lower-profile Jewish friends in East Hampton thought of a temple at the Borden estate. "At the entrance to town?" they said to him. "Jews running around in their *yarmulkahs* and their prayer shawls! Who needs to start trouble! Evan," some told him, "We'll give you money *not* to build it!" That, so goes the story, convinced Evan, as if he needed any convincing, to go through with his plan.

When Markowitz and Zeldin returned, Evan took them to the Borden estate, walked them up to the house, past a copper beech tree of epic age and beauty at the entrance, and offered the property to the Jewish community as a grander and more appropriate house of worship than the one he had been shown in their plans. Markowitz and Zeldin were delighted, not only with Evan's suggestion, but because Jacob Kaplan had also agreed to share equally with Evan the cost of launching the Jewish Center. Kaplan matched the price Evan paid for the property with a fund to refurbish the building and to render it suitable for worship.

Although for the High Holidays of 1959 and 1960 services were held in the Session House of the First Presbyterian Church of East Hampton, the future of the Jewish Center of the Hamptons was now assured. Evan, Jack Kaplan, Joseph Weinstein, and a number of others were elected trustees in June 1961. And on August 10, *The East Hampton Star* reported, "The first Jewish community center in the 300-year history of East Hampton, the Jewish Center of the Hamptons, now in its first real home at 44 Woods Lane, will also have its first permanent rabbi."

It was a satisfying Rosh Hashana and Yom Kippur, 1961, for Evan. Instead of going into New York to be with the family at the West Side Institutional Synagogue, he was in East Hampton, now his real home. He particularly enjoyed the way the rabbi, Albert Friedlander, conducted a special High Holiday service for children, who sat on the grass beneath the mammoth branches of the copper beech. This tree, among the noblest in East Hampton, had attracted Evan to the Borden estate the first time he saw it. There is some vestigial nature worship in all religions, and Evan, with his intense love for trees, land, and woods, was showing himself to be a kind of Jewish druid.

There were two bittersweet ironies that did not escape Evan's notice in 1961 as the Jewish community moved into the house he had provided. First, when the founding families came in with mop and brush to clean, they found a large number of anti-Semitic tracts in the rooms of the Borden estate. This, however, was balanced — if such things can be said to have balance — by the good will of one of the Temple's most eminent neighbors, Paul Tillich, who lived in the house just to the west on Woods Lane. A well-known religious philosopher who left Germany in 1933 when Hitler came to power, Tillich became friendly with Rabbi Friedlander. This distinguished philosopher once said, "I had the great honor and luck to be the first non-Jewish professor dismissed from the German Universities."

In the 1960s the travel bug had bitten Evan again, and he toured Scandinavia. Then he went to Thailand. In time, he began to take extended winter holidays in Jamaica, often in the company of friends like Leonard and Margot Gordon. While these were primarily pleasure trips, they were also informal art-buying trips. A sophisticated but impulsive buyer, who carried photographs of his garden in his pocket, like snapshots of family, Evan began to bring back sculpture that appealed to his eye, his fancy, his sense of humor, and his nostalgia. He returned from Italy with copies of two Roman gladiators to hail his guests as they made their way to the pool. He purchased the sophisticated compositions of the Israeli Menashe Kadishman and of Fritz Wotruba. From a primitive Jamaican "Henry Moore," Evan commissioned driftwood carvings that were copies of the great master's early work. Then, placing the completed sculptures not too far from an original Moore he had purchased for his garden, he enjoyed the irony, and was amused by the oohs and aahs of unwary admirers.

For Evan the purchases were only an initial installment on the greater joy of planning the placement of the pieces, often in surprising settings in the expanding labyrinth of the gardens. The placements — in the curve of a path, on a grassy slope visible from the house, before a berm of lilac, or in a secret alcove of trees — were at the heart of the garden and its spirit, a kind of exterior expression of Evan's mannerist and essentially playful aesthetic sense.

Sometimes on Evan's travels, the young Gordon children were along with their parents. Since Evan had known Margot's mother at dances at the Sea Spray in the 1940s, and had squired Margot about East Hampton before she married, he used to joke that he had now lived long enough to romance three generations in the same family! In fact, there may actually have been a few instances when that exaggeration was no joke at all!

"Several times I have been to Evan's house," recalled José

Tasende, a close friend and art dealer whom Evan met in Acapulco, "and there were two or even three generations of women present. Evan had had an affair with them all — grandmother, mother, and daughter! But I am not surprised, because he has dedicated his life to living intensely, and what is there more intense than sex and love!"

It has been said of exceptional people like Evan, who have lived rags-to-riches lives, that no matter how polished they become, they allow to surface, later in life, some peculiarity or eccentricity. However, with his Manhattan moorings cut and his lands and reputation on the South Fork growing, Evan made the transition from being a strong and flamboyant personality in the business circles of New York City to being an exceptional character in a small town. And he did so while avoiding, by and large, the pitfalls of eccentricity. He, of course, now donned his English deerstalker cap, secured the brims fore and aft, and tied up the earflaps. Then he threw on his Balmacan or his Inverness cape, and, using his knobby cane solely to point out topographical features to visitors, he took his dog, Misty, and walked the land.

Whenever he acquired new acreage, Evan always walked it over and over again, as if the physical contact, all the clearing away of brush, all the chopping down of dead branches, all the thinking about how the land might be improved, was the rite through which the land became his in a manner more real than the exchanging of money and legal papers. He was continually laying plans to highlight a copse of scrub pine, to make a glade romantic, or to move or re-position several huge boulders that a glacier had unthoughtfully pushed onto his property 10,000 years ago. Evan found promontories for the farthest views or the best path to take across a field, and he visited and revisited them with guests and friends. Always, he was thinking about the land.

If this activity, or his costume, were eccentric, then so be it! This is what a landowner did. If on these thousand and one walks he took Evan imparted to an accompanying friend like Joe Weinstein or José Tasende a story of his own landless growing up or a Jewish joke, then that was as it should be, too. For Evan fancied himself — and he was and is — a country gentleman, and a Jewish country gentleman to boot! If our colleges bestowed noble titles instead of the degrees *honoris causa* that would come to Evan later, in the 1980s, he well might have been dubbed Sir Evan Frankel, Squire of East Hampton (which is what people were calling him anyway!). No knighthood would have fit better or been better earned.

Evan's most unusual public activity was neither his Sherlock Holmes garb, which he wore both for comfort and, he freely admitted, cachet, nor his walking his lands, but his uninhibited displays of affection for women. By the mid-to-late 1960s, the curving female line already occupied prominent and honored places in Evan's sculpture garden, and he was as attracted to living females as he was to their varied representations. Friends joked that he always had a blonde on his arm. This interest, however, masked an attraction beyond the sexual. For there was also a re-charging of the life spirit, an incomparable *élan vital*, by turns libidinal, aesthetic, and maternal, that Evan absorbed from the beautiful young women in his life. In return, he often played a very significant role in theirs.

Among his friends, at parties, whenever his naughty flirtatiousness inspired him, Evan's hand might move toward an unguarded breast the way a meteorite, once in her gravitational pull, makes toward Mother Earth. Accepted, humored, slapped, or rejected, Evan took his chances. He did so in part because his aim was to do precisely as he pleased — especially on the grounds of his own home — and in part because he was always intrigued by how far limits and decorum might be strained by inserting a certain acceptable risk into a social situation. The enemy of a good time, according to Evan, was not outrageousness, but boredom, and he provided the sparks for many a memorable afternoon and evening. Let the Comstocks gossip about him if they chose. And they did!

IX

An *enfant terrible* socially, in his real estate affairs Evan kept a much lower profile. Occasionally he spun off one property in order to buy another, more frequently than not upzoning the property when possible. He never advertised or put up a sign, and he absolutely never sold land to builders or developers. Not to do so was Evan Frankel's eleventh commandment, and his lifelong observance of that real estate commandment would be exemplary. It was his chief instrument to inspire others to preserve East Hampton's unique beauty. Evan might break, as we all do, some of the commandments one to ten, but the eleventh never! To avoid the pitfalls of mistaken development, Evan Frankel was a crusader, a true *Evan*gelist.

In fact it was that passionate belief that made Evan's tenure on the Village Planning Board increasingly stormy and enormously frustrating for him. In 1963 the sudden boom in land values, especially East Hampton woodlands, was leading to unprecedented land sales and a consequent surge in subdivision and development. The officials of the village and town of East Hampton hired outside consultants to formulate the Comprehensive Plan. "Upzoning" — the raising of the minimum legal lot sizes to build on — soon became everyone's byword.

Anyone familiar, however, with the issues at stake between builder and land investor, local resident and weekender, preservationist and developer, knows that to attain fair and orderly growth that satisfies all interests is extremely difficult and never a matter of good guys versus bad guys. To address such complex problems as population density, traffic control, water resources, and the maintenance of a community's identity called for compromise and cool heads. Evan believed that public forums and political debates were not the only or even necessarily the best way to promote such balanced thinking. Another way was Evan's way, that is, by setting an example, as these excerpts from the minutes of the Village Planning Board reveal:

— June 29, 1964:
Mr. Evan M. Frankel, who owns fifty or more acres in Parcel 3, proposed for upzoning, volunteered to have his holdings changed to Zone A.

— July 14, 1966:
Mr. Evan Frankel suggests that recreational areas be established in all future subdivisions.

— February 1967:
In discussion of the Egypt Close developer's map, Evan Frankel commented that the Planning Board is within its legal right to demand open space. However, since the developer had provided several 2-acre lots already, the effect of open space would be achieved without resorting to legal means, and this should establish, Mr. Frankel said, a precedent for the board's future considerations in dealing with developers.

— April 8, 1967:
Mr. Frankel said he thought it would be advisable to have an Architectural Board of Review. If the citizens wanted such a board now, they should act, he said, and not wait until the property owner had made plans and a public hearing held.

— April 13, 1967:
Mr. Frankel, in answering a citizen's question as to how such thickly-settled subdivisions as Egypt Close might be prevented in future, said, 'If it were the province of the board to demand more, we would have.' He said it was 'only by the grace of God that there were not 40 houses going up instead of 20. Of course,' he said, 'there are always people who think a half acre is plenty. I personally think five acres would be better!

There were a few humorous moments in these otherwise arid minutes of an increasingly stressful decade. In August 1968, one board member, Charles Osborne, suggested that he agreed with Evan about a matter but he might change his mind if Evan didn't stop talking! Evan, fixing on him an orgulous stare, asserted he would continue talking and in fact wanted to talk at some length "about upzoning philosophically." After a brief discussion, the board agreed to table Evan's philosophical discussion of upzoning until a later date.

Of Evan's role on the Planning Board during this period, writer Berton Roueché, who was chairman of the Joint Town and Village Planning Board, summed it up best: "Evan was one of the earliest to lead the way in how not to abuse the land, and he deserves much credit for that. He may have pontificated a lot, but he was always on the side of the angels."

It was at this time, in the summer of 1967, that twenty-three-year-old, lustrous Elena Prohaska, the daughter of Evan's friend Ray, entered Evan's life.

Just as he had reached out to Peggy Goldsmith when he was forty years old, now, at his next major chronological plateau, sixty-five, Evan turned one day to Elena, whom he had known since she was a child. "Look, sweetie," he said, "let's you and I go traveling and enjoy life. Why, in fact, don't you

161

move in here with me? I'm tired of living by myself!"

Evan, who had made such proposals before, was perhaps a little incredulous when, after some deliberation, Elena accepted. She moved into Hither Lane, and the yellow room at the top of the steps soon became known as "Elena's room." Her graceful features and dark hair, her refreshing simplicity and unadorned beauty were all reminiscent both of Peggy Goldsmith and of Evan's mother.

To Evan, Elena and her youthfulness were a kind of "Life Force,'" as woman perhaps had always been to him. To Elena, Evan was like the magus in the John Fowles novel of the same name, which she had been reading the day Evan made his proposal. "He was that character, the magus, come to life," she recalled. "It's a very engimatic older man who takes younger people on journeys —part real, part surreal — during which they have to discover who they are. And when it's over, they end up where they began, but wiser. Of course, I knew Evan's reputation in East Hampton. Every girl did. But the real Evan has this wonderful magical quality. The real Evan is also pixieish, and with a touch of the devil about him." Between being on the side of the angels, as Berton Roueché had described him, and having a touch of the devil, Evan Frankel, as usual, had all bases covered!

And indeed Evan and Elena traveled far together. There were many trips to places Elena had never visited. Evan delighted in being her guide. On one memorable journey, they went first to Florence, then to Rome. There Aldo Gucci, whom Evan had met in 1950 through Menotti, entertained them. Their next stop was Geneva, and later they were off to St. Moritz, in the company of their friends, the Bigars. In London Sarah Churchill was their hostess. Still later came Dublin, Ireland, and Dramoland Castle, where they were searching for sculpture in the uproarious and impious company of Irish writer Ulick O'Connor. They also often visited Montego Bay or Acapulco in the wintertime. In Mexico, they stayed at beautiful Las Brisas overlooking the Pacific. Through José Tasende they discovered the sculpture of Francisco Zuniga, which Evan began to collect in earnest for his garden.

But always they returned to Hither Lane, or, beginning in 1968, to Evan's apartment at 5 Riverside Drive. Elena used the terrace apartment as her New York City headquarters when she began to study art history at New York University Graduate School. The explosive days of 1968, full of student protests and drug busts, made the world seem even crazier than usual. Elena's parents, who adored and respected Evan, approved of the arrangement, feeling their daughter would be safe with Evan.

Of course there was talk of marriage between Evan and Elena, but both knew that would have ruined what had become their mutually supportive and loving relationship. José Tasende, who has a fine appreciation of the enigma who is Evan, put it this way: "Evan's gregarious spirit and his need for human contact contrasts sharply with the isolation that he has chosen to live in." Evan ultimately loved to be unencumbered, and the unavoidably messy daily routine that marriage entails would, Evan feared, strip the relationship of its zest and joie de vivre. His life with Elena was rich, indeed, but also full of a new and troubling possessiveness, and even pain, that was — that is — part and parcel of the conjugal state. To live with someone, to marry, means to tolerate the push-and-pull of the heart, and Evan had decided long ago that he preferred not to tolerate but to live and enjoy intensely. In 1975 Elena and

Evan parted. They remain friends, and Evan still reminds her that he gave her the best years of his life!

It was fortunate that Evan's many friends and relatives always stayed close to him. For, although he was now past the allotted three score and ten in excellent health, many people close to him were already gone. John Small had died in 1962 and Harry Green in the following year, and their passing grieved Evan terribly. His oldest sister Annie had died in the late 1950s. Baby sister Claire was dead, suddenly, at age fifty-nine in 1964. And the deaths, in 1969, of both Harvey Fite and Seymour Gross were great blows to Evan. Ten years later, Evan would give one hundred acres, his last remaining lands in Woodstock, to the Opus 40 Foundation, in memory of John Small.

Fate had more blows for Evan, and within one very bad year, 1970 to 1971, Evan's brothers Aaron and Dave and his sister Yetta died. Within three weeks of Dave's death, his daughter Anita Kessel, whom Evan was very close to, lost her five-year-old boy Todd in what should have been a routine operation. Evan was the first to arrive for the funeral, and he saw that his niece could not bear to stay to receive guests. The accumulated sorrow was too great. "Evan said to me," Anita recalled, "'Just leave here and come with me to East Hampton.' The day after the funeral we left. And there Evan was the greatest comfort, because he simply let us be. We were there for two weeks, and in the beauty and quiet of Evan's place, it was easier to bear our grief."

There is no sorrow sharper or more disconcerting than the death of younger relatives and friends. Perhaps it was for this reason, as well as the need to use his talents, that Evan had, by the late 1960s, thrown himself into a number of new and important projects. Although still a member of the Village Planning Board, for some time Evan had been exercising considerable private diplomacy in the dining rooms and on the patios of East Hampton. This could take the form of a genial jibe or a ranting fulmination over cocktails, urging his neighbors to act in concert in resisting developers. In September 1968 a pet project Evan had been working on for years came to fruition. Most of his fellow property owners along the ocean between Indian Wells Highway in Amagansett and the Maidstone Club signed a voluntary agreement pledging themselves not to build south of the second line of dunes for fifty years.

While this was a victory for the pure conservation of precious Atlantic oceanfront, it was also a vindication of Evan's oft-stated proclamation that "people are more touched by example than rhetoric." Nevertheless, the pace of development was quickening in the village and town of East Hampton. Most property owners, unlike Evan, could not afford to hold on to their land for long periods of time. Never was it clearer that the question now was no longer development or no development, but rather what kind of development. Would it be shortsighted or farsighted? Evan's conversion of his Newtown Lane commercial properties was an example for others. He had purchased a former garage, and now boutiques flourished, so that the whole street retained its character while similar sites in neighboring Southampton had been turned into commercial strips. Evan had, once again, justified his philosophy. He told the *Star*'s reporter, "tender handling of property pays off rather than flash-bang development."

Evan now scouted about, looking over the land for just the right property where another example might be set. He was searching for an impressive way to demonstrate to the commercial developers coming into East Hampton how a person might make a good profit while at the same time respecting and retaining the beauty and character of his home town.

He finally settled on a twenty-three-acre parcel on the Pantigo Road. From 1924 to 1943, the acreage had been the East Hampton Riding Club, which had disbanded during the second World War. Now for over twenty years, potatoes had been grown on the land, and the stables and barns had been used for potato storage.

Working with Amagansett contractor Tom Nesbitt, Evan set about converting the barns into a series of interconnected boutiques. A new roof on one barn, a foundation over the dirt floor of another, air-conditioning, a sprinkler system, a fresh coat of paint, and soon the five gray-shingled buildings were ready for use. Evan, of course, also did extensive and careful landscaping, and brought in seventy-five shade trees, so that when finished, the buildings were hardly visible from the highway. However, they were inviting and interesting, and never was there a parking lot more serenely graced by trees.

Evan stipulated that the buildings be used in an as-is condition, and eventually Sterns Department Store accepted the challenge and rented the space. Soon merchandise was hanging from the low-raftered ceilings and was heaped in wicker baskets that lined the wooden walls. It was the natural beam and floor look of today, far ahead of its time. The store manager joked that this was not a branch of the company but a twig, and *The New York Times* headline joked "Store Takes Root on a Farm on Long Island," but everyone was happy, and everyone was making a profit.

It was a business and aesthetic triumph of the first magnitude for Evan. He was positively strutting with pride. Who else would have been able to remodel stables and barns and then entice a multibillion-dollar corporation to accede to his concepts? Evan's young friend Ed Bleier, a kind of official squatter-in-residence in one of the barns when it was being refurbished, said, "Evan set out to show that property could be respected and still be good retail space. This was Evan's aesthetic/preservation sensibility and his commercial sense working beautifully in tandem." Or, as Evan himself put it: "I wanted to say to people, Look, you can make money, you can have stores, but you don't have to put up some cheesey crap. Besides," he added, with a whimsical gleam, "it was really fun to have a shop inside a barn instead of a sterile box."

And yet if Evan's example set a precedent, not everyone was willing to follow. Right down Pantigo Road from Sterns there were a number of what Evan called "horrors" already going up. As the 1970s neared, therefore, issues on the Village Planning Board were becoming heated. There was also a significant new player, for pressure was being applied from newly formed grass-roots citizens' groups, alarmed, highly informed, organized, and impatient with the plodding pace of the legal and political process.

Evan was impatient, too. Parking at Main Beach was overflowing onto private properties, and Evan publicly declared the village was "in a pickle" due to bureaucratic bungling and lack of planning. He disqualified himself, in November 1969, from voting as a Planning Board member on a zone change from residential to commercial to permit a Gristede's food store on Newtown Lane, because his properties fronting Newtown Lane could benefit. He spoke out, however, as a private citizen to oppose the plan because of the traffic problems it would cause and the bad precedent it would set. When a commercial developer sought the removal of the 1799 Lyman Beecher house at Main Street and Hunting Lane and requested rezoning for commercial purposes, Evan declared his personal vociferous opposition. A week before the Village Planning Board was to discuss the matter, Evan told the *Star* that enactment of the plan would be a sacrilege tantamount to destroying the entrance to the village. In 1970, during another controversial meeting of the Village Board on parking restrictions at Two Mile Hollow Beach — where Evan, in the 1950s, used to ride and swim virtually alone — he bemoaned the drastic change in the character of the beach. "We won't preserve the beauty of the village," he declared with angry alliteration, "with a shimmering mass of molten cars. We all came here to get away from that!"

By the spring of 1971, Evan had already developed a reputation for such eloquent outrages, expressed at public forums when, in his estimation, the beauty or character of the village was at risk. He said more than once, with the truth of simplicity, "We are in love with this place!"

Evan had by no means cornered the market on concern for the area or on outrage or public speaking. However, his stature as a major, wealthy, and civic-minded landowner, and his moral and financial support of Citizens Concerned for East Hampton and other grass-roots groups combined with his slot on the Village Planning Board to make people — and the press — stop, look, and listen when Evan Frankel cleared his throat and made his way to the podium.

There was also Evan's gift for oratory. Absolutely no one in town could "philosophize" about upzoning quite like Evan. And he had no peer when addressing an adversary with nineteenth-century theatrical bombast or confusing one with sesquipedalian phrases. After all, Evan was seventy years old, a child of the pre-microphone era of William Jennings Bryan and Teddy Roosevelt. Morever, by now he felt that his contributions to village life had earned him the authority of an elder statesman. Indeed, he was something of the male equivalent of his dear friend Jeannette Rattray, who was one of the *grandes dames* of East Hampton. Evan was perhaps a *grand seigneur.* Evan therefore provided, when he rose to speak, not only leadership, but often also a good show.

There was something else: publicity. No novice to promotion and publicity from his business life, Evan still had a great knack and even a love for it. He knew that reporters covering developments in East Hampton could personalize their stories by hanging them on his colorful head. Evan, in his numerous interviews, therefore, was always careful to be quotable. One has the feeling that when replying to a reporter's question, he was not merely answering, he was also speaking lines he had been mulling over, not only for a particular interviewer, but perhaps for future voters and even generations. Of course, he enjoyed the spotlight, but he almost always used it to speak less of Frankel the man than about Frankel's policies and the light they might shed on pressing issues.

And yet, even as much as two decades after Evan's arrival in East Hampton, misunderstanding lingered. Writer Morton Hunt, who had bought eight acres from Evan, interviewed him for *The New Yorker* and grilled him about his motivations. It is worth quoting from the 1968 interview at some length, because Evan summarized his history, as well as the state of his heart at the time. Hunt wrote:

I suggested that perhaps he had been as much motivated by potential profit as by his love of beauty. He abruptly lost his look of beaming bonhomie and became severe; indeed almost angry, "I *deny* that," he said. "I *deny* that. I saw this as one of the most idyllic, peaceful areas anywhere near the city —a place of unspoiled beauty, rusticity, and colonial charm. It had beach, village, countryside, all in one — and all less than three hours from New York. But it was in mortal danger. The land had been sold off by its original owners during a couple of booms back around the first World War and in the early twenties. Most of it, when I got here, was in the hands of people who didn't care about it, but who regarded it as an investment and wanted to resell it at a profit to a developer, as soon as possible, or to cut it up and develop it themselves.

"Along I came, a man who fell passionately in love with the land and was determined to keep it unchanged as long as I could. Little by little, I acquired acreage — the boom prices had collapsed during the Depression, and had never come back — and I held onto most of it. Over the past twenty-five years, I've accumulated about a thousand acres, six hundred of which is in farmland, the rest in woodland. My background has given me an insatiable hunger, a special neurotic need to own land. I enjoy nothing more than driving around, looking across a sweep of beautiful land, and reminding myself that it's mine. But you see what has happened. People call me a land hog, a monopolist, for refusing to sell them land so they can ruin it with their abominations, their cheap, tasteless developments, their ghastly neon lights. They call me a profiteer, an exploiter, who's holding out only so he can make the maximum profit!"

In fact Evan had never been against profit. Profit was important and essential to reasonable development, and he had demonstrated that. No, he was, as his friend Leonard Gordon described him at the time, like the reputed Hawaiian missionary: "He wanted to do good *and* to do well at the same time." To Evan the real enemy was not profit, but greed.

If Evan was misunderstood, it was due in part to the flamboyant, high-flown vein in which he often spoke his mind, a style that could be seen as pretension. It might also have been because Evan had done so well; his success invited envy. Perhaps his Jewishness was also a factor. Finally, Evan may have been misunderstood because he was, he is, an original, and an original always makes the most demands on perception.

Elena remembered how the increasingly tense Village Planning Board meetings were taking their toll on him. "Evan would literally be sick when he returned from some of them," she said. "He would enter shouting, 'Those bastards! That sonuvabitch! That moron!' There was an undertaker on the board at one time, and Evan was convinced that the man's primary interest was in bringing more bodies to East Hampton!"

If the vision of officials was, in Evan's estimate, Lilliputian, much of it was a result of the recession that afflicted the country in the early 1970s. Although elements of a Comprehensive Plan were already in place in the village, there was also a need, it was deemed, for rapid local business expansion. Since some sort of commercial district for hotels was also rec-

171

ommended in the plan, in 1971 the village fathers published a legal notice of a proposed hotel-motel zone in which the owner of ten or more acres anywhere in the village would be permitted to erect up to two hundred twenty motel units on it.

The storm of protest this notice unleashed was compared to the hurricane of 1938. On June 23, three hundred people jammed the VFW Hall for a public hearing to denounce what had come to be known as the floating hotel-motel zone. Many groups, like Citizens Concerned for East Hampton, and private residents opposed the plan, and Evan, by design, was the last speaker. His remarks were short and eloquent: "I'm the largest landholder in the village. I stand to profit the most from this proposal, and I say, To hell with it! It's a Pandora's Box that will mean the destruction of a three-hundred-year-old village that we've all tried desperately to preserve."

When the rousing applause subsided, Evan demanded an immediate poll of the people present. An enthusiastic "Nay" reverberated through the hall, and the village trustees took a brief recess. When they returned, they voted not to adopt the proposal.

It was a resounding victory for the principle of democracy in action, but it also underlined publicly that on the Planning Board, where he had always been something of a maverick, Evan Frankel was now truly odd man out. Because of that, he would soon be officially out. In the fall of the following year, he was not reappointed to the Village Planning Board. That was *not* quite democracy in action.

What brought this about was the next bitter imbroglio before the board, in May 1972. It was a proposal for forty "Village Towne Houses" on eight acres in the northern portion of the village. This was the first proposal for "cluster" housing in East

172

Hampton. Calling for exceptionally dense development, it envisioned, among other things, multistory structures on a third of a tract of land in exchange for keeping the other two thirds in open space. Emotions were running very high.

Sitting in his chair as a Planning Board member, Evan, who deeply opposed the plan, upbraided the large protesting contingent of "Towne House" neighbors for trying to close the barn door after the horse was out. The *Star* recorded the session as one of Evan's "eloquent tirades," and then noted that a very large dog, having gained entrance to the packed Village Hall, began to bark nastily at Evan during his peroration. Like the cadaver in the funeral parlor in Manhattan, perhaps that dog's ferocity was a kind of omen of the political move to come.

When the vote was taken, at the end of May, four board members voted to approve the $1 million "Towne Houses." Evan Frankel cast the only "No."

If the 1960s were idealistic and cantankerous, the 1970s were growing nasty and litigious. Frustrated by their defeat, the "Towne House" opponents sued the Village Planning Board in June, claiming that the project broke zoning ordinances. On the heels of that, a builder also sued the board for the right to build "Pondview," a proposed development of thirteen building lots on seventeen acres adjacent to Guild Hall. It was the last piece of undeveloped land in the heart of the village. Evan took up the fight, criticizing the project repeatedly in executive sessions of the Planning Board. He urged the board at least to reduce the permitted number of houses from thirteen to eight. Evan recollected, "I had to walk out of one meeting when I was verbally attacked by another member."

Time after time Evan watched worried local business people facing off against a growing ecological/environmental watchdog movement, with the politicians caught in between and playing catch-up. Not a political person himself, the more political and confrontational the atmosphere became, the more unhappy Evan was on the board. Moreover, things were not much more amicable down, or up, the Montauk Highway. As Evan cast his eye to the east, he saw a plan to convert the vacant Montauk Manor to a Hilton Hotel, and the yacht club into a luxury resort. He looked west and saw a proposal for a thirty-unit condominium at the former Mecox Bay Duck Farm and a 152-apartment complex across from the Southampton Golf Club.

In July 1972, to protest these "horrors," as its first newsletter described them, the Group for the South Fork was formed. The group's language and outrage were Evan's language and outrage. So, although he sat on the Village Planning Board, his heart was with this organization of people who, like him, were — as one member suggested — girding their loins because East Hampton was being violated. He agreed with the group's purpose, as proclaimed by its director, Ian Marceau, "to offer techniques to provide jobs, growth, and a balanced society, with a salubrious environment." Evan was at the first meeting of the group at the home of his neighbor Tassos Fondaros on Further Lane. Never temperate in opposition to actions of the board he thought too favorable to developers, Evan, in the company of these like-minded people at this inspirational first meeting, let out the full depth of his feeling. According to the *Star's* reporter, Evan called some of his fellow village officials "ignorant, stupid people."

Therefore, Evan was not surprised when the Village Planning Board discovered an overlooked ordinance that required the current board to be dissolved and a new board to be appointed. When this action was taken in November, Evan was not reappointed to the post he had held for nearly two decades.

The brouhaha that followed Evan's firing filled the *Star's* front page. Village Board members publicly ducked answering questions about why Evan was not reappointed, and the usually wry and restrained *Star* reporters listed the various locutions stonewalling took: "I have no comment whatsoever on it." "I have no reasons for anything." "They just appointed these gentlemen." "I wasn't at that meeting, had to leave after five minutes." "I have no idea."

Evan knew why. "It's perfectly obvious," Evan said at the time. "What do they want a guy like me always opposing them? They want a controlled board." He predicted that the new Planning Board, whose composition was weighted with businessmen, boded ill for East Hampton's future.

X

It was time for Evan to take Voltaire's advice and cultivate his own garden. And what a garden it had become!

In twenty years, by 1967, Evan had transformed his fifteen acres into a green and whimsical wonderland. There was an impressively eclectic sculpture garden, and beyond it an array of winding paths, with unexpected turns, views, flights of fancy, waterfalls, pools, and bamboo groves. An elegant young female nude by Zuniga stood at the entry to the swimming pool, directing guests to the water. A bust of Evan looked down on the shenanigans, and at the far end of the pool there was even a miniature copy of Claude Monet's bridge at Giverny. The Henry Moore reclining nude had her own little alcove of privet hedge nearby. Everywhere were landscaped settings in which Evan had positioned his sculpture — ancient and modern works, originals and reproductions — with romance, drama, and fun.

In the mornings, Evan sat on his terrace, shaded by an overflowing arbor of bittersweet, and conducted his business by phone. From here he could see his graceful Zunigas and his Pompeian girl. Beyond were the many new pieces he had acquired: a white dove of peace by Jane Wasey, a marble fountain originally given by the Vatican to the American ambassador in Rome, and stone *putti* representing music and the arts. On the main rolling lawn behind the residence was a formidable concrete head from the old Ziegfeld Theater. Nearby was another steel and glass construction by Kadishman, new pieces by Amy

Small and works by Amerigo Tot and Bridgehampton sculptor Warren Padula.

The major new element in the garden, however, was the work of Albert Price, whom Evan hired as a gardener in the early 1960s. Inspired by all the sculpture on the grounds, Albert — without Evan's knowledge — began to sculpt primitive figures in wood. Albert was a former West Virginia coal miner, with no formal artistic training, but he had been born to the American mountain tradition of whittling. From boyhood, he had the rare, native talent in his hands. At first he used the root ends of Dutch elm-diseased trees, often thrown down by storm and tossed in the town dump. With the bark gone, and deeply weathered, the wood was treated with a preservative. It soon had the appearance of gray stone, only soft, by comparison, and ideal for carving.

One of Albert Price's first pieces was "The Spectator," which Evan at first placed in a kind of literary juxtaposition with his two embattled gladiators. Encouraged both by his Springs neighbor Willem de Kooning, and by Evan, Price carved statues of classic subjects, starting with mother and child. But soon he also was doing humorous and fantasy subjects, individual portraits and groups, made of both wood and metal. Many were tailor-made for his boss. Price, for example, sculpted figures of Evan's friends, the Bronfman family, complete with the components of a charming little still. Near the bamboo grove, planted a dozen years before, and now fifteen feet tall, Evan placed many of Albert Price's new pieces. Out of an old boiler, Price made, at Evan's request, a miniature locomotive for children to play on. Nearby was a humorous and monumentally bespectacled head of Governor Nelson Rockefeller, fashioned from a discarded building ventilator. By 1975,

Price had not only sold dozens of his sculptures locally, but he had received a commendation from the Smithsonian Institution and was on his way to being an exhibited, successful artist. Albert Price's second career not only imbued Evan's garden with a new and distinctive element that fit perfectly with the other fine follies there, but it also represented an artistic version of the rags-to-riches fantasy come true. It was more than fitting that Evan had discovered Albert Price and promoted him.

Evan began every day by walking the gardens, because the gardens and the grounds were like his children, and he had to see to them right away. However, real children came, too. There were the Frankel grandnieces and grandnephews, some of whom worked summers in the garden. Their families came to visit, too, and the families of friends, and schoolchildren by the classful. Groups from Guild Hall and other local institutions also came for the tours of his garden that Evan loved to give. He often ended the tours in a special children's area, where the centerpiece is a large playhouse bounded by bamboo jungle on one side and a huge fallen climbing tree on the other. Inside are many toy sculptures and caricatures, some by Albert Price, some found treasures, but all enchanting.

In ways only Evan knows, the children's area — its bamboo-lined paths leading to fence-less white gates that mysteriously beckon, enticing entry into the next vista or landscape — is perhaps the source of the unique spirit animating the whole estate. Full of the child's sense of the lovely and the magical in everyday things, this was the private wonderland of every child who visited, and it has remained long in many young visitors' memories. Mysterious and on a scale larger than life, as if a Lewis Carroll dream fantasy had suddenly materialized on Long Island, the children's area expressed Evan's extraordinary empathy for children and the profound belief, which is at the heart of all childhood, that you can indeed go anywhere you want to go, be anything you desire. That, after all, was precisely the fantastic life Evan was leading.

The thousand and one tours Evan gave of the estate, the screeching peacocks welcoming him home at night, the grand entrances at the Spring Close restaurant, where the maitre d', George Polychronopoulos, addressed him as M'Lord! — these were among the elements that enhanced the role Evan had written, produced, directed, and was now starring in, as the Squire of East Hampton.

His nephew Ernest told Evan that he might have been one of America's greatest actors. On the stage of East Hampton, Evan was certainly a star. And soon his New York City and Long Island notices began to come in: The headline of a *Newsday* article about Evan read "Outrages of M'Lord," and *The New York Times* called him "Lord of East Hampton Manor." However, if the eloquent outrages of "M'Lord," were an act, Evan told one interviewer in 1975, it was always one with a purpose. "I ranted and raved," he said, "but never without getting right to the mark. I also did it for effect. There's not enough passion in the world. This is what you have to do to get anything done."

As to his being a character at age seventy-three, Evan also could reflect from the tranquility of his garden: "I sometimes put on a flip surface because it's the best way to carry things off. Get too serious, and people shy away from you. If you're not mundane, you're a character. A character is a guy who doesn't want anything, who's full of fun and life and vivacity. A character is a guy who has land and won't split it up into small pieces. It's sad that I should have to be so different because I'm doing all the right things. Do the wrong things, and you're no character!"

Evan's garden was a refuge for him, but he never allowed it to cut him off from responsibility for the care of a larger garden, the beautiful community in which he lived. In many ways, Evan's recurrent public theme, his big issue, had always been what he called "ambience." His goal was to beautify his environment, or, as he sometimes put it, in the negative, "to campaign against uglification." In 1968, another champion of beautification, Lady Bird Johnson, had invited Evan to attend a ceremony in the White House Rose Garden. Evan and the First Lady exchanged notes and press clippings, and he left with a heightened sense of the value of his example.

Since he could no longer be an advocate of good taste and sensible development as a Planning Board member, and because East Hampton in 1972 experienced the second highest growth rate of all towns on Long Island, Evan took on new responsibilities. He went to work to strengthen those local civic institutions that embodied the traditions of art and beauty at the very center of East Hampton life, Guild Hall and the Ladies Village Improvement Society.

A long-time champion of Guild Hall's John Drew Theater, by 1968 Evan was also very active at Guild Hall's museum, lending his collection of Marisol sculptures for an exhibition that year. The following year Evan was working hard on the fund-raising committee for Guild Hall's new wing. That summer, and for many before, Evan also was friend and advisor to Ann Light, chairwoman of the Ladies Village Improvement Society. For years an Italian donkey cart Evan owned had been a fixture, overflowing with books to sell, at the society's summer fair, its most important fund-raising activity. In the early 1970s, as the society's need for space increased, Ann Light asked Evan for use of one of his properties on Newtown Lane. Evan happily complied, and the fair's Bargain Bookshop was born. The revenue from the fair's book sales more than doubled that first summer, and each summer thereafter. "Evan," said Ann Light, "always opened his house, his garden, his grounds, and his heart, if anyone asked him to do something for the town. But if someone was trying to exploit East Hampton, watch out! Because Evan Frankel had no patience for that!"

Evan's collaboration with Ann Light was yet to have its finest hour in connection with the East Hampton Free Library. Jeannette Edwards Rattray, a library board member, publisher of *The East Hampton Star,* and a great friend of Ann Light's and Evan's, died in May 1974. She was, in the words of her eulogist, the poet Jean Stafford, "East Hampton's most assiduous historian and ardent panegyrist." Although Jeannette Rattray and Evan had come from different worlds, they shared many qualities of the spirit, including great presence, a supreme individuality, and, most notably, a profound love and allegiance to the village. In recognition of her long association with the library, a fund was established for a permanent memorial in the form of an addition to the library. Since the cost of a large new addition appeared to be prohibitively expensive, the library's Advisory Board was considering a small new working area for the staff as the addition in honor of Mrs. Rattray.

When Evan heard this, he grimaced. Jeannette Rattray was not small, but large and majestic, and just as the original humble design for the Jewish Center had not sat well with him, the idea of a modest staff addition did not seem appropriate to Jeannette Rattray's spirit. Ann Light picked up the story: "Evan admired Mrs. Rattray very much. He loved the idea of doing something for the library, which Jeannette had loved, and the more we talked, the more a public wing in her honor became a splendid idea in Evan's mind. Even though I told him that the library board had already said that, although it was a beautiful idea, the cost of a wing was estimated at a prohibitive $200,000. But Evan, who always thinks big, said he had already been thinking of giving $5,000 to the Ladies Village Improvement Society for trees in Jeannette's honor, and he would start the ball rolling by giving that toward a new public wing for the library.

"Well, when the Library Board and its advisors met — the Library Board is all women but we have an Advisory Board of businessmen — and I re-proposed the idea, they reiterated that it would be impossible to raise $200,000. So I stood then and said, 'I have $5,000 to start it right here.' And I said, 'I think we can make it $10,000 without any problem. I know it's not impossible because I've been told so by someone and I believe him, because he's never been wrong yet.' They were impressed, but I kept them in suspense for a while, and then they finally asked, 'Well who says it's not impossible?' And I answered, 'Evan Frankel.'

"'Evan Frankel!' they responded. Well, the facial expressions of those men began to change, and they started then and there to rethink their position on the matter, because everyone knew what a good businessman Evan was and that when Evan said he was going to do something, he was!"

Evan was asked to join the Advisory Board, and he sparked the fund-raising. In December 1974, plans for a $195,000 addition, the Jeannette Edwards Rattray Memorial

Wing, were announced to the public. By mid-January 1975, $50,000 had already been raised; by July the drive was at its midpoint, with over five hundred contributions, and on schedule with half the money raised. In September, with $30,000 left to go to reach the goal, ground for the wing was broken. In May 1976, less than two years after Mrs. Rattray's death, the new Jeannette Edwards Rattray Memorial Wing was dedicated and its doors opened. It was a remarkably swift and successful effort, because of Jeannette Rattray's unique standing in the community, and also because of Evan's involvement. "It would not have happened without him," Ann Light remembered. "This was why the men on the board looked a second time when I invoked Evan's name, because he was known as a man who makes his visions come true."

Making visions come true, however, is hard work, and Elena recalled Evan's days in the late 1960s and early 1970s: "People were constantly coming in for advice, asking him questions, picking his brain. And he would answer them all. He would talk to anybody. He was very, very generous that way." Whenever he and Elena went to lunch at Gordon's restaurant, Evan was still on the job. Lunch was never just lunch, and dinner was rarely a purely leisurely meal either. Evan was working. Each meal outside of the house was, depending on whom Evan found in the restaurant, a kind of spontaneous unplanned fund-raising collation. "And Evan," Elena said, "was continually table-hopping. 'What are you running for?' I used to ask him. 'For office?' The answer, of course, was that he was continually raising money for some East Hampton cause."

In Elena's jest, there was, however, truth. Evan wasn't running for office, although he might have done so. His name was by now a household word in East Hampton, which, despite its growth, was still very much a small town. Everyone had an "Evan story," had heard him speak at a meeting, had followed his real estate career in the papers, had spotted him driving his red Jeep near the beach, had seen him over the years, a strong physical presence, swimming or chasing girls in the surf, or had seen him more recently with cape and walking stick moving briskly toward his land. Or they might have glimpsed Evan early one remarkable morning in 1973 walking with his houseguest José Tasende, like a renegade sabbath-rule-breaker out of East Hampton's venerable colonial past, calling up to the bedroom windows of his Hither Lane neighbors inquiring if husband and wife had fulfilled their connubial obligations the previous night!

No, Evan wasn't running for office; he was already *in* office: he was the Squire of East Hampton, the Lord of Brigadoon, its knight-defender checking, good-humoredly, on the status of his lands, crops, and vassals, and collecting not rents, as squires and bailiffs might have done, but contributions to the library, the Ladies Village Improvement Society, Guild Hall, and — very soon — the Jewish Center.

Like any good lord, Evan's advice and wisdom were often sought out. In 1974, Joan Paley, divorced from Barney Straus (grandson of Nathan Straus) — but not without honoring Evan as godfather of her two children, Barney, Jr. and Tracy — was considering marriage to Joseph Cullman. Joe Cullman then was Chairman of the Board and Chief Executive Officer of Philip Morris. Joan remembered Evan's advice to her at the time. "It's not good to marry a man with a jet plane of his own," he told her, "unless it's taking you where you want to go."

It turned out that it was, and with the additional good fortune that Joe Cullman now entered Evan's life as a new and valued friend. And he and Joan included Evan in all the important events of their lives. In Joe, Evan saw a man in the mold of his early best friends, Harry Green, John Small, and Emerson Thors. Joe was enormously dedicated to business but at the same time committed in his philanthropy, his leisure interests, and his love of wildlife and the environment. Perhaps most of all, here was a man, a star of the corporate world if ever there was one, who also brought humanity, tenderness, and even humility to all he did.

Perhaps it was Harrie Ellen, Harry Green's daughter and another of Evan's godchildren, who sensed the most profound ground of Evan's regard for Joe Cullman. "There was a side of Joe Cullman," she recalled of this time, "that to my mind is like the soft side of Evan himself, a side that he often finds difficult to express or prefers to keep hidden. It was the rare person," she went on, "like Joe who would spar with Evan, listen to him take an outrageous posture, and then patiently and methodically outline how he felt Evan was wrong. But the very best part was when they'd finished sparring. Joe then put his arm around Evan, and off they went for a walk."

The following year, in December 1975, Harrie Ellen herself married. Evan gave his goddaughter in marriage to Tom Schloss, a caring, thoughtful man who had the gift of instantly sensing Evan's fierce independence and his vulnerabilities. Tom's ministrations during the most dangerous nights of Evan's illness twelve years later were absolutely essential to Evan's recovery.

Evan had known Harrie Ellen from her birth, and since the death of her father, Evan had been in many ways her living link to him. Her relationship to Evan ranged from the child's natural attachment and awe to that of a college student stagestruck by all the celebrities in Evan's life, to that of an adult.

186

One of the most remarkable qualities that Evan possessed was the flexibility to change and to embrace Harrie Ellen, Joan, and many others, as they grew or changed in varying personal, social, and even business relationships with him over thirty, forty, and sometimes fifty years. The heart of this rare flexibility was that Evan always knew, in Harrie Ellen's apt phrase, "when to let the past determine the present and when to let the past be reflected in the present."

If this flexibility was one reason why so many people have been drawn to Evan and have stuck by him, there was another reason, too: his aura of theatricality. When Evan walked into a room, when he was on, the play had begun, the atmosphere crackled with excitement, and people around him, from every social station, were suddenly actors. Evan's theatricality was so irresistible because it tapped the secret that we are all, to greater or lesser extent, merely actors, playing the role of Self in the drama of our own lives. As Leonard Gordon once put it, "Evan is like all of us, only wonderfully exaggerated."

Tom Schloss, who came to know Evan late but well, suggested that the source of this theatricality was Evan's keen, if often inexpressible, awareness of vulnerability — his own and that of others. When harnessed or converted, that awareness took the form of an active energy that was, Tom recently said, "so concentrated and so available that you may be drawn to it, or driven from it, but to which it's impossible to be indifferent."

In 1975, Evan gave up his apartment at 5 Riverside Drive. It had been more or less only a *pied-à-terre* for the past ten years. If New York had any charm left for him, it was no longer alluring enough to merit a place to hang his hat. East Hampton had everything Evan wanted.

* * *

Alas, it seemed, it had everything everybody else wanted, too. The huge five hundred fifty-acre Bell estate was on the sales block, and subdivision was imminent. The town, which had given the go-ahead to an oceanfront development, was now being sued for allowing subdivision on primary dunes. Weekend traffic was as heavy as midtown Manhattan's at midweek. Yet in the bicentennial year, 1976, local builders were vehement in defense of their American heritage: the right to make any reasonable use out of their property, and the new ecological purists be damned! In a disturbing session of the East Hampton Town Board in December 1976, newly elected officials certified that they were not now, nor had they ever been, members of the environmentalist Group for the South Fork.

As Evan approached his seventy-fifth year, he was personally feeling fine, but, as he put his fingers on the pulse of East Hampton, he sensed growth was approaching fever pitch, and the diagnosis was not good. As a man who always looked ahead, Evan had to give thought now to the future of his land. He had held onto it for thirty years, with the result, as he said, that "because I didn't develop it, I was a community hero to some, but because I wouldn't sell the land, I was a sonuvabitch to others." He liked the praise, to be sure, and he had learned to ignore the criticism, but his focus now, at three score and fifteen, was to make sure he passed on the stewardship of his lands to people who felt as he did and would continue the tradition.

Because he wanted others to follow his example, he let it be known just what kind of buyer he would consider: "The people to whom I sell are not interested in subdividing," he said. "They've got enough money to hold onto the land they buy. They're not out for a fast buck. Also," he explained for those who did not appreciate the public service performed by the enlightened private landholder, "what a lot of people don't understand is that the man to whom I sell a large amount of land will not be a threat, but an aid to the community. He places no imposition on the people living here year round. He pays a huge amount of taxes to the town. He has a private road the town doesn't have to maintain. His children are in school elsewhere so he puts no burden on the school system. In addition, he provides employment for three or four people on his property alone, and he spends thousands in the town's centers of commerce."

So Evan began to find people and they him: his friend Ann Light, president of the Ladies Village Improvement Society; her daughter Deborah Perry; the Rockefeller family; Andrew Sabin, a young businessman with considerable land holdings, exceptionally strong environmental interests, and with a special regard for Evan, in whom he saw the feistiness of his own father, who was also a battler from the Lower East Side. To these people and others Evan gradually sold large tracts of the most beautiful woods and farmlands. He told the buyers — and they understood — that the transaction was not a simple sale. Evan was conveying the land into their trust. Between Evan and his buyers there were always either extraordinary meetings of the mind about preservation of the land or actual covenants written into the agreements of sale. The parcels either were not to be developed at all, or, by stipulation, might have only a house or two on them. Sometimes, if he could get away with it, Evan put height restrictions on building sites. With truth in the heart of his jest, Evan said to a reporter, "I make my own zoning."

Once, however, in 1974, a friend begged Evan to sell him an acre amid long, rolling, uninterrupted potato fields. Evan resisted, but the friend was insistent. "Who are you, God?" he said. At some point Evan relented, with the sorry result that on that horizon a stark modern white house, unrelieved even by trees, soon was obtruding upon the sky. "That was my first mistake," Evan remembered, "and I hope my last."

The closings of Evan's sales, the principals remembered, were quite extraordinary. Although sizable amounts of money were changing hands, there usually were very few questions, no suspicions, no certified checks. By the time Evan was ready to transfer stewardship, there was usually so much good faith accumulated that the closing was less a legal proceeding than a ceremony of trust performed with a shake of the hand or even a celebration. "After you bought land from him," Deborah Perry remembered, "Evan would suddenly appear and visit it and still take others to see it. Why? Because it was beautiful and he continued to care about it after he sold it. Evan was tremendously pleased when the land I bought from him — wonderful Bridgehampton loam — became part of the county farmland preservation. When Evan and I see each other we always smile because he knows I won't sell even one clod of the land."

XI

As Evan divested himself of his properties, one might have thought it in the regular course of events for him to become less involved with East Hampton. But the regular course was never Evan's. He continued to be more involved than ever in local institutions, and among them the Jewish Center occupied a unique place.

Through his 1960 gift of the Borden estate, Evan had become a kind of godfather to the Jewish Center. He had helped at its birth, and therefore, although his involvement during the years since then had not been on a daily basis, his interest was keen and far more than solely philanthropic. As a trustee, he was very proud of the place, praying there on the High Holidays and on the occasional sabbath. Whenever he set foot in the Jewish Center, it felt like home.

In 1964 the Center numbered thirty-five families as members and boasted its first *bar* and *bas mitzvahs*, Philip Markowitz and Marlene Richer. The families divided into committees that year and painted the temple themselves. It was still hard at times to field a full *minyan*, a quorum for prayers. Irving Markowitz, the president, and Evan used to joke that the only way to get the Jews on the south side of the Montauk Highway to come out for the High Holidays would be for Evan to drive an antique car down the lanes while Irving blew the *shofar* to wake up the sleepy co-religionists.

But Evan had other, more practical, ways. He recruited among his friends, using the time-honored Jewish arts of guilt and blackmail. He invited his new friend Leonard Gordon to celebrate Yom Kippur, 1964, at the Jewish Center. When Leonard turned him down, saying he wanted to relax and Yom Kippur was like work to him, Evan said, "Look, go to services and I'll call your mother and tell her you have an *aliyah* and she'll be proud of you, and you'll make her happy." When Gordon still resisted, Evan said, "If you can't go, I'm going to call your mother anyway, and tell her you're not only not going to services, but you're also playing baseball and, because God doesn't want Jews to field fly balls on Yom Kippur, you'll maybe break your ankle, too!" This had actually happened to a mutual friend the previous year when the artists-writers ball game fell on the High Holidays.

Leonard Gordon still resisted. Then, in Leonard's words, "Evan actually picked up the phone and dialed my mother in Florida. 'Debbie,' he said, 'How are you? I've got wonderful news for you. Your son is going to have a special *aliyah* at our Yom Kippur services!' He was really locking me in. So naturally we started going to the Jewish Center. Here I was, a thirty-seven-year-old man and Evan had called my mother and blackmailed me into going. I loved it so much, I later became president!"

The year Gordon assumed the presidency was 1987. By then, the Center had grown so much that the large tent brought in for Rosh Hashana and Yom Kippur was filled past its one-thousand-person capacity. However, twenty years earlier, perhaps only seventy-five or a hundred worshippers could be mustered, and sometimes, in the absence of a cantor, Evan or Charlotte Markowitz dug up a vintage recording of Yossele Rosenblatt singing the Kol Nidre service. The standard joke at the time was that to have a regular *minyan* at the Center one would have had to include in the count the Markowitz's dog, a lovable mutt, over age thirteen, of course.

The Jewish Center was from the beginning a warm, intimate, family place, and between 1964 and 1974 it grew under the leadership of presidents Markowitz, Zeldin, Sy Karp, and Charles Egosi. There were annual dinners and dances, and awards given by Evan to honor the outstanding man, woman, boy, and girl of the year in the Jewish Center's family. There was a children's summer camp, which Evan particularly liked to visit. There were also exchange programs with Israel, activities for teenagers, and a solid adult education lecture series.

This was a real place, a focus for Jewish community life. Evan's pleasure in the growth of the Center was augmented by the pride of having helped to create a Jewish institution where none had existed before. Moreover, they had done this in an American town that was once less than welcoming to Jews. At the time of Evan's arrival in East Hampton in 1946, a Jewish Center would have been unthinkable. This knowledge gave Evan intense satisfaction and a measure of private vindication. His philanthropic work on behalf of Guild Hall or the East Hampton Free Library or the Ladies Village Improvement Society did not provide Evan a joy anywhere akin to this.

And Evan knew it, as did his family and close friends. Emerson Thors joked wryly — as Evan gratefully pocketed his check for the Jewish Center — that Evan's work on behalf of the Center was practically the only good thing Evan had done in his whole life! Although others expressed amazement at his growing involvement with the Jewish Center, Evan was not surprised at all. It seemed to him the most natural thing in the world. He always saw himself as a committed Jew, although he was not regularly observant. It had just taken the right opportunities for him to express himself fully.

In 1967 Evan was elected a trustee for life of the Center. For the next several years, he wrote a fund-raising appeal with goals in keeping with the modest size of the Jewish Center. Although he was only warming up for his major effort ten years later, people took notice of the particularly focused vigor, passion, and purpose Evan brought to fund-raising. When it came to the Jewish Center, Evan Frankel did not want to be turned down.

By the early 1970s, the congregation had outgrown its space. With second-home ownership rising dramatically, limitations of the seventy-seat sanctuary and the absence of a reception area were causing increasing problems for a Center dedicated to opening its doors to all worshippers. There was not enough space to accommodate both weekend and year-round people. For large occasions, such as a *bar mitzvah*, or when the High Holidays fell on the weekend, tents had to be pitched to accommodate the crowds. But everyone knew this could only be a temporary solution.

In 1976 plans were drawn up, and a fund-raising drive was begun to build a sanctuary of adequate size. Two days of heavy rain in October underlined the urgent need for action, for the weather made it impossible to erect a large tent to accommodate the expected four hundred people for the Yom Kippur service. Frederick Schultz, the minister of the East Hampton First Presbyterian Church, came to the rescue. Evan, Leonard Gordon, Irving Markowitz, and Rabbi Silverman loaded the Torah scrolls, pointers, and prayer books into the back of a station wagon, and off they went, along with the congregation, to the Presbyterian Church's Session House. The Kol Nidre service, on Yom Kippur eve, 1976, was chanted in a church that had provided the Jewish Center, yet again, in the words of the eighteenth-century English hymn, "shelter from the stormy blast." Robert Osborne, one of the elders of the church, was reminded by this occasion that when the church began its own building fund drive, the Jewish Center had been the very first contributor.

On the balcony, as the Kol Nidre worshippers filed out, the Reverend Mr. Schultz exclaimed, "My God, Evan, how do you do it? Even when there's a flood, you have more people here than we do."

"In that case," Evan replied, "why not consolidate? You become good Jews, and I'll be a mighty good Presbyterian!"

The experience solidified the ties of ecumenism and good feeling binding one of the oldest with the newest religious institution in East Hampton. It also underscored for Evan and the other Center leaders that enlargement and renovation of the sanctuary could not be deferred.

The first plan was for an extension directly behind the sanctuary, a sort of chapel annex with a cement slab reception area in front of it. Evan felt that would not be at all in keeping either with the building he had given the Center or with East Hampton, and, as always, he spoke his mind at a board meeting. In matters of building, grounds, or architectural taste, few people were willing to buck Evan. The main part of the plan was therefore dropped, although the concrete patio was eventually laid to anchor the tents brought in to shelter the overflow of people on crowded holidays.

Perhaps to offset the concrete in back, Evan encouraged his friend, the local artist Arline Wingate, to contribute a large sculpture of an *aleph* — the first letter of the Hebrew alphabet. With the sculpture and the copper beech both gracing the grounds of the Center, Evan had, it seemed, brought together for himself the things that mattered to him most: art, nature, the Jewish community in East Hampton.

In January 1977, Evan turned seventy-five. He was still fit as a fiddle and had not been sick or inactive a day in his life. Joan Cullman sent out birthday party invitations featuring a picture of Evan in his Inverness cape. As the guests arrived for the celebration, a smiling, larger than life cutout of Evan himself greeted them at the door. There was something very apt about this theatrical prop, because Evan was indeed a local celebrity. He had around him a circle of the most interesting and devoted friends, all of whom agreed that Evan was surely at the top of their "Most Remarkable Person I Have Ever Met" lists. And in East Hampton, Evan's celebrity status was exceeded by no one. No less a judge than George Polychronopoulos, whom Evan had encouraged to open the highly popular Gordon's restaurant, said: "In East Hampton Evan Frankel was — and is — it! Out here there are millionaires and multimillionaires, and very famous people, actors, writers, artists. I remember vividly when I was maitre d' at Spring Close, Willem de Kooning was at one corner, table 14, and Evan was in another corner, at his regular table there, table 9. De Kooning got up, walked over, and said hello to Evan. That kind of encounter happened dozens of times. Now a thousand celebrities come to Gordon's, and absolutely no one is as well known as Mr. Frankel."

Among the seventy-fifth birthday gags and tributes, none was better than Emerson Thors's affectionate and hilarious verbal "roasting," *Evan M. Frankel — From Gas to Riches*. Reproduced and distributed by Frank Farrell to all of Evan's many friends, Emerson's S.J. Perelmanesque chronicle captured both the spirit of that memorable evening and the zesty friendship Evan inspired:

Evan M. Frankel —

From Gas to Riches

As Evan's oldest friend, I have known this greatest source of natural gas this side of Oklahoma since his earliest adultery. So the time has come tonight when I must explode the highly volatile myth.

Seventy-five years ago today, in a very posh mountain ski resort — Zermatt — our friend Evan M. Frankel first saw the light of day, at night, in a luxuriously appointed Chambre à Coucher in a Louis-the-Fourteenth Château. There, in his little blue-ribboned bassinet, surrounded by his eight brothers and sisters, Mama and Papa Frankel beamed on the second coming of the Lord.

In youth, Meshulam was the recipient of costly private tutelage in music, ballet, painting and the classics, including karate. Better to provide these amenities Papa Frankel, moonlighting from his rabbinical chores, organized a chain of Salons de Massage in the friskier resort cities of Europe.

Instant success crowned the family endeavor in which Meshulam had a monopoly on the towel and chewing gum concessions. This caused the local gendarmerie to arrange promptly for Papa and the Frankel famille to pack up and junket to America in a deluxe suite aboard the luxury liner Queen Elizabeth.

In his early adolescence, Evan was influenced by Palladio and decided to study architecture under Le Corbusier and Frank Lloyd Wright. This prepared him for his entry into the world of big business fronts. The firm of Ross Frankel Inc. was

197

Evan's creation and its original designs and drawings were the formats later usurped for the Word Trade Center.

Having made his architectural mark early, and having absolutely no interest in making money, he threw himself into other areas of activities. He worked indefatigably at Clancy's Tub in the Bowery, the Salvation Army, and the Visiting Nurse Fund. Later, changing pace and faces, theatrics absorbed his attention, and he shared his thinking and creative dreams with John Houston, Irving Thalberg, and Gian-Carlo Menotti. He directed and produced The Medium by telephone. And, with the Alfred Lunts, Louis Sobel, and Zero Mostel, Evan laid a solid foundation for the Theater Guild and the Hippodrome. His intimacy with Churchill, Truman, and the Maltese Falcon made Frankel an international character. Since then, the name Frankel has always reminded everyone of some sort of character.

However, his total modesty and timidity were his greatest problems. He was ultra-shy, withdrawn, introverted, introspective, and given to moods of great silence. He had little ability to express himself and, when he did, he recorded his every word on tape.

What other pleasures could this unsure soul have? He had no interest whatsoever in women, though he longed inwardly for their companionship, which, fortunately for them, he never found.

In real estate he couldn't have cared less, though infrequently he made a nickel here and there. Then what? Through his early training in music and the classics, he turned to ballet and bought himself a tutu that he shamelessly wears with regularity, even tonight, under his Sherlock Holmes outerwear.

Being completely camera-shy, the only chance his friends

or the press has of catching Frankel on film would be during the early morning hours — when he breakfasts in his aviary with his peacocks and Chinese hens — which merely confirms the general opinion that he's really for the birds.

Happy, Happy 75th, Paps. See you on your centennial.

XII

Before his centennial, however, Evan had at least one more big job to do. He was determined to build in "America's most beautiful town" America's most beautiful Jewish temple. It was a tremendous job for a seventy-five-year-old man to undertake, one which, although he did not know it at the time, would absorb him for the next ten years. The new sanctuary of the Jewish Center of the Hamptons, to be called the Gates of the Grove, was to be Evan's crowning achievement. But crowning achievements are arrived at only after a journey of many, and sometimes arduous, steps.

It began in June 1977, when at a time of dissension on the Center board, Evan acceded to a request from Bernard Zeldin, like himself and Jack Kaplan a trustee for life of the Center, to stand for president of the congregation. As Betty Marmon, secretary of the board, recalled the moment, "On the board at the time there were several personalities in conflict. Evan was seen as not part of any one of the arguing groups."

For that reason, and also because Evan was Evan and he wanted to preserve what he'd helped to begin, he ran, and won. From that time on, Betty Marmon worked closely with him. "When Evan took over," she has said, "it was not seen as the beginning of a new chapter. But things definitely calmed down when he took the helm."

The chief issue at the Center was the same as in East Hampton, in microcosm: growth and planning. By 1977 the Center had reached a membership of one hundred thirty families. Because growth was inevitable, the questions were: How much growth? What kind? What size should the Jewish Center be? What, moreover, should be the Center's religious style, scope, and image in the general community? Was it both a religious and a social organization and, if so, how much of each? Moreover, could it effectively serve both the local year-round community and the growing and influential second-home owners? In a phrase, what was to be the vision of the Jewish Center of the Hamptons for the current generation and those to come, and how did all that fit in with the growth of East Hampton at large?

It was no secret that Evan Frankel had a few ideas on these matters. What was clear to all, however, was that no new building or sanctuary renovation could be sensibly undertaken without first resolving these questions. Although Evan proceeded in a gingerly way and with the usual committees, his assumption of the presidency of the Center was in itself already the resolution, or a major step toward the compromise required for growth. For one way to give an institution vision — often the best way at a critical or disputatious juncture — is to imprint the institution with the vision of one charismatic fellow. Evan was not by nature an administrator, but a leader. Or as Evan formulated it, "To do things in a highly personal way was the only way I knew how to do them."

From the beginning, Evan was a hands-on president with two chief goals: first, to maintain harmony by promoting a temple for all worshippers regardless of economic or social status, place of primary residence, or whether they preferred more or less Hebrew in the service; second, in its growth, renovation, building program, and in all the Center's activities, to maintain the very highest standards.

In the fall of 1977, a recently widowed congregant asked Evan to have a tree planted in her husband's memory. Her request was the catalyst for an idea Evan had been considering. Shortly afterward, he conceived the Jewish Center's Memorial Grove, a serene retreat behind the sanctuary where congregants might have a tree planted and dedicated to a departed or living friend or family member. Evan, with customary fervor, began to raise money for this memorial arboretum, proving, as his friend José Tasende suggested, that the new temple president was at heart pre-Abrahamic, a nature-worshipper, an idolator of wood and trees — something of a Jewish pagan. Perhaps. The grove, however, was also Evan's simple, loving gesture toward his large family — brothers, sisters, nephews, nieces, other relatives, and friends — whom the years were taking away from him.

Evan was also deeply moved, as was all of East Hampton, by the untimely death of Jeannette Rattray's forty-five-year-old son Everett, the *Star*'s popular editor. In Everett Rattray's poignantly stoical obituary, which he had written himself before he died of cancer in December 1977, there was much to admire. He wrote that the unusual name of Rattray had led some of his classmates in school to think he might be Jewish. He didn't mind that one bit, he said, and he'd also had difficulty in finding a Presbyterian minister to marry him because his bride, Helen Seldon, was Jewish. And, lastly, when it came time to decide details of his burial, Everett Rattray had inclined toward cremation, but his wife, "who had lost," he wrote, "many, many of her relatives to such flames in Eastern Europe in the 1940s, prevailed, and pine-box burial was arranged in a peaceful and private spot."

Because of his longevity and the large size of his family

and circle, Evan was experiencing and would continue to experience more than his share of such sadness. The Memorial Grove was Evan's way of fulfilling the deeply felt, natural desire to gather near to him, in a beautiful setting, those he loved. On the level of membership-building, which he never lost sight of, it was also an astute idea in its own right, a kind of temporary surrogate for a Jewish cemetery.

On Friday nights, as he took his seat as temple president on the *bemah* behind Rabbi Albert Silverman, Evan did so with consummate pride and ease. It seemed as if the seat had been carved specifically with him in mind and had just been waiting for him to fill it. Evan was not only the temple president but also its patriarch. As he said in many different ways, it was a demanding job, but one that gave him much in return, not the least of which was the opportunity to reclaim fully, although in a different fashion, the world of his father.

Regularly Evan spoke after the rabbi's sermon. After the rabbi introduced him, "And now our president, Evan Frankel, has a few words," Evan strode to the lectern and welcomed the congregants and potential new members. He commented on the rabbi's sermon and then almost always integrated into his remarks variations on the themes and leitmotifs of his own experience growing up Jewish. He spoke of the world of the Lower East Side, the early immigrant days of poverty, the sweatshop *bar mitzvah*, and the underlying theme throughout was the crucial role of community as a palladium for Jewish ethics and values, then and now.

Returning from his winter vacation in Jamaica, in March 1978, Evan submitted to the Center board tentative studies for a new sanctuary to adjoin the present building as well as a complete renovation of the current structure. At the July annual meeting, the Jewish Center members were to review these plans and to vote on a resolution to amend the Center's constitution. The purpose of the amendment was to create three additional trustees, whom Evan strongly felt were needed to help him in fund-raising to implement the plans. When the resolution failed, by only four votes, to get the required two-thirds majority, Evan did not hold his fire. He told the congregants he thought there was a danger of the Center getting mired in a habit of thought that was failing to come to grips with the future. He called the reasons offered to defeat the measure "irrelevant and fatuous" — one always knew where Evan stood. He admonished the congregation that fuller cooperation was needed, and he vowed to carry on. And he did, concentrating in the summer of 1978 on what was immediately achievable. As trees and flowers bloomed, he worked to enrich the landscaping and to bring the Memorial Grove to final form.

In the meantime, however, Evan was needed on still another board. In late summer, not long after he returned from his brother Irving's funeral, Evan was elected to the board of trustees of Southampton Hospital. It was the first of several civic honors that were to come his way. Now that, of all his siblings, only Phil and Mayer were left, he was more aware than ever that he, too, was approaching octogenarian status.

With most honors come also responsibilities. Evan, however, knew precisely where his chief responsibility now lay. His sights were firmly fixed on the Jewish Center and the community building he had undertaken. Therefore, on Yom Kippur, the Memorial Grove was dedicated. In a special Yom Kippur ritual first conceived and conducted by Evan in 1978, and now a tradition, those who have planted trees in the grove go there before the *Yizkor*, for a memorial service that is surely unique in American Jewish life. As chamber music plays, the congregants gather in the grove, and when they are assembled Evan greets them with poetry. He reads from the local writers he admires, such as poet John Hall Wheelock, or he chooses a selection from the Victorian writers, such as "In Memoriam" by Tennyson. The rabbi and cantor chant the blessings and then read off the names of those remembered. As each name is read, the benefactor steps up to receive a flower from Evan's hand.

That first service was a great *succès d'estime* for Evan. Twenty-five people participated, and the numbers grew each year. The other High Holiday services were also moving and packed to capacity.

The Center was very much back on track. A year later, therefore, in August 1979, the resolution to add three new board members passed handily, and Evan was poised to begin fund-raising in earnest for the addition to the sanctuary. Evan's optimism could be sensed in the monthly messages he sent to the congregants in the fall of 1979 and spring of 1980, bulletins that surely have no peer among those of American temple presidents in the horticultural pleasures they evoked: "Our gardens are ablaze with brightly colored mums and other fall blooms," he wrote, "and give much pleasure to our members, passers-by, and the entire community. . . . The shrubs and privets, too, are freshly greening, gladdening the heart and restoring the soul. . . . Our Memorial Grove trees are changing their leaves now into multicolored living canvases, a testament to the beauty that surrounds us." Evan's "living paintings" were alive and well, only now he had not only found them, but in the precincts of the Jewish Center, and particularly the grove, it was as if he himself, finally, had painted them as well.

Everything was moving along swimmingly. Attendance at Friday night services rose and fell with the seasons, but that was to be expected of a congregation with many summer and weekend people as members. Springtime had definitely arrived in the life of the Jewish Center, and it was ready to bloom. There was a Sanctuary Building Fund and a Memorial Grove Maintenance Fund, and under Evan's leadership and that of the Center's treasurer Stephen Spector, the Center was enjoying, Evan wrote in a letter to congregants, "a fiscal health that would be the envy of any organization, including that of our own United States."

Perhaps most satisfying of all to Evan was the ambitious new summer camp for young children begun by Stephen Spector's energetic and dedicated wife, Karole. From the beginning it was a spectacular success. That first summer Evan went often to watch the small children do arts and crafts or act out stories from the Bible. The scenes of children at play in the camp or pronouncing the blessings at the Center's model *seders* in the spring, he told his friends, were all the reason he needed to keep up his efforts. For Evan, a man by choice without wife and children, the Center was becoming like another cherished garden for him, a real kindergarten, where he wanted to be sure Jewish heritage and values were being planted, harvested, and passed along for the future.

Then trouble struck. Rabbi Albert Silverman tendered his resignation. The reasons he gave were personal. He wanted more time to pursue his teaching and to resume his law practice, and he had just remarried. Yet, when a congregation's rabbi resigns, the consequences are almost always public. Evan tried to dissuade the rabbi from his decision, but to no avail. Rabbi Silverman conducted the High Holiday services in mid-September 1980, under a large tent thronged with worshippers, and then he left the pulpit in October.

Even a Jewish center with as energetic a president as Evan Frankel needs a spiritual leader, particularly if the congregation is vibrant and changing and full of Jews of different backgrounds, modes of worship, and differing degrees and styles of Jewish identification. The Jewish Center had been growing evenly and steadily, but now, poised to make the quantum leap of growth that the new building represented, it found itself without a rabbi.

A little furor, fed by anxiety for the future, developed in the wake of the rabbi's departure, and congregational morale fell. Maybe all the plans for growth, said one group of congregants, were too ambitious for a village that was still essentially a resort. After all, none of the churches in town were trying to embrace the summer Episcopalians or the summer Presbyterians. But the Center was reaching out to all the Jewish people who summered and spent weekends in East Hampton, from artists to financiers, to the whole economic and social range. Maybe a little universe of Jews with so much heterogeneity simply could not be happy under one temple roof, no matter how architecturally splendid it would turn out to be. If, as the old joke goes, two Jews always have at least three opinions, perhaps Evan's dream was not realistic. If Adas Israel, the temple in Sag Harbor, once had its congregants grow so angry at one another that they erected an iron fence to divide the graveyard into two, who knew what might occur here?

Some members left the Center. Evan, who did not like an atmosphere that had lost its harmony, and who realized that such an environment was poison to the fund-raising efforts necessary for growth, tried to put the best public face on the matter. He wrote a letter to the congregants "From the President," which concluded with his opinion that compared to the *sturm und drang* of the national election of 1980, the Center was doing quite well. "Our Center," he wrote, "is moving forward on a cohesive course toward solid growth in a spirit of amity and devotion to our faith."

To insure that that would indeed happen, Evan and the board of trustees began with dispatch to interview rabbis. In January 1981 they engaged David Greenberg as interim rabbi, to fulfill the Center's needs until a congregational meeting could be held in June. At that time it would be determined whether to retain him or to seek another new rabbi.

While the search committee comprised Evan and several other temple members, it was primarily Evan, as temple president, who was responsible for the choice. Characteristically, he converted a moment of disarray, which might have become a full-blown crisis, into an opportunity. As Evan began to know David Greenberg, he realized that here was not only a seasoned and highly literate rabbi, but also a man who was by nature a peacemaker. Furthermore, David Greenberg had been coming to the East End for summers since the 1950s and, like himself, was utterly in love with the South Fork. From personal experience, Rabbi Greenberg knew that for families like his own, twenty or thirty weekends of first-rate family time plus several weeks in the summer on the South Fork were sufficient to create, over the years, a wealth of memories and a profound attachment. And where there is memory and attachment, there is the emotional *sine qua non* for genuine community.

The most impressive growth of the Jewish Center of the Hamptons had up to now been visible during services on crowded Friday nights in the summer and, especially, on the High Holidays where the tent size, like the cuffs on the trousers of an adolescent, had to be let out and increased each year. If the local community could, without fear of losing its identity, truly hitch its star to the growing community of second-home owners, the Jewish Center of the Hamptons might grow, in Rabbi Greenberg's words, "into its full responsibility as a congregation." As they talked, Evan realized that here finally was the partner he needed to launch the Jewish Center of the Hamptons into its maturity.

"In the beginning," Rabbi Greenberg recalled, "Evan may have been the slightest bit hesitant about making the new leap. After all, he was nearly eighty years old when this major building effort was undertaken. He could have rested on his laurels, because he'd given the initial building and grounds. He could have chosen not to risk tarnishing his reputation in his eighth decade by being associated with a temple whose future direction was still the subject of some squabbles and some uncertainty. But the Center mattered too much for Evan to rest."

As Evan and the rabbi discussed the pros and cons of growth, including the raising of significant funds for the first-class building that would definitely make the Jewish Center of the Hamptons far more than a small-town temple, Evan realized that the job would be primarily up to him. "Once committed," remembered Rabbi Greenberg, "Evan was absolutely the engine who drove us. Without him there would have been no new building, no full service Jewish Center of the Hamptons."

In June, Rabbi Greenberg was appointed. The next month he and Evan presided over a symbolic groundbreaking ceremony, marking the opening of a fund drive for the temple addition. The Attorney General of the State of New York, Robert Abrams, was the principal speaker.

If you want something done, says the old apothegm, ask a busy person to do it. In June 1981, Evan was also elected to the first of two three-year terms as a member of the board of trustees of Guild Hall. His election was most appropriately timed, for 1981 was Guild Hall's fiftieth anniversary. There were four major art exhibitions of East Hampton artists, six plays at the John Drew Theater, and a host of other activities marking the transformation of Guild Hall from a modest community center into a dynamic regional arts institution. What Guild Hall had also come to occupy over the years, in the words of *The New York Times* reporter, was an "unusual mediating position among the artists, the local residents, the wealthy summer colony, and the new wave of New York visitors." Such a broad scope also seemed to describe, in a personal way, the aims of Guild Hall's newest trustee. Morever, such a unifying embrace was also an apt characterization for what Evan and Rabbi Greenberg were now trying to accomplish at the Jewish Center.

Although it would increase Evan's burden measurably, the decision was taken early on that, for the sake of harmony, temple members would not automatically be assesssed for contributions to the building fund. This unusual policy was rare in the annals of American Jewish temple-building. At the season of giving, Hanukkah and year's end 1981, Evan underscored this approach in his message to congregants. He wrote that his solicitation was going to continue to be "personal" and low key.

Personal, yes. But, if Evan's fund-raising was low key, then Hurricane Gloria was but a breeze.

A fund-raiser is, like a salesman, an exceptionally adroit

persuader, and Evan's whole career, including his recent warm-ups with Guild Hall and the library, had, in a sense, prepared him for this campaign. "I've seen the very best of fund-raisers," said Andrew Sabin, "and not a one of them can hold a candle to Evan Frankel in action. He asked me to get involved with the Jewish Center two minutes after we met."

When an old business acquaintance stepped out of Evan's past and into an elevator at the twenty-seventh floor of the Carlyle Hotel in Manhattan, Evan talked so fast and so well that the fellow had committed $50,000 to the Jewish Center by the time he stepped out, shakily, only four floors later. Someone joked that every time Evan went to lunch or dinner at Gordon's, a red warning sign should have been placed on the sidewalk near the restaurant entrance, reading: Danger! Fund-Raiser at Work. Enter at Own Risk.

When his friend Frank Farrell, an Irishman, gave Evan a check for $5,000 for the temple, Evan turned it into a fund-raising tool superbly crafted and sharpened to induce a little pang of healthy guilt when carefully applied to a prospective donor. Evan carried the check around so long, brandishing it before Jewish East Hamptonites still reluctant to support the Center, that months went by without his cashing it. In time he had to return it, dog-eared, to Frank and ask for another to be issued.

Evan good-humoredly acknowledged that in matters pertaining to fund-raising for the Jewish Center, the Squire of East Hampton had, in some quarters, become the Scourge of East Hampton. In the winter of 1982, in his holiday message to congregants, Evan wrote, "Your president has been devoted to the task of raising funds over the last year for a new sanctuary. In the course of this serious and arduous task, there have been some lighter moments. He has earned the title of 'Solicitor General,' 'Beggar in a Buick,' and 'Prince of *Schnorrers*,' among other sobriquets.

"Valuable prizes," Evan went on, "will be awarded by your president for any new and apt titles you may come up with to describe his fund-raising activities.

"He has also been enjoined when invited to a dinner party to refrain from a high-powered pitch for the Jewish Center. He has been called upon for innumerable contributions to causes ranging from saving Galapagos reptiles to skiing scholarships as a *quid pro quo*. Your president has taken it all in good stride and he and the sanctuary fund have both thrived."

Evan was thriving indeed. On May 23, 1982, in his eighty-first year, dressed in his stylishly fraying finery, his eyes bright with concentration, his bearing proud and erect, Evan attended the commencement exercises of Southampton College of Long Island University. He was not there to attend the graduation of a grandniece or nephew or that of a grandchild of one of his many friends. On this bright May afternoon, Evan Frankel himself was about to receive a degree.

Long-ago memories of City College, New York University, Columbia, and scholarly paths not taken must have stirred Evan as Henry Purcell's "Trumpet Voluntary" thrilled the air and the academic procession entered. They moved toward the stage to the strains of "The Earl of Oxford's March," which Evan, that Oxford don *manqué*, also particularly enjoyed. In the company of painter Jimmy Ernst and nuclear scientist Bernard Manowitz, who, along with Evan, comprised the pleiad of recipients of honorary degrees, Evan's achievements were recited:

The fields and beaches of Eastern Long Island are precious to us as our legacy to the long future. It is a quality of Evan Frankel's protean intelligence that this knowledge motivates him as a designer, builder, and landowner to make conservation of this beautiful place a guiding principle. . . . He is an art collector of impressive acuity. . . . He is deeply engaged in the cultural and religious life of his community. . . and serves on the Advisory Board of the East Hampton Free Library and the Board of Directors of South-ampton Hospital; he has been President of the Jewish Center of the Hamptons since 1977. We make obei-sance to those who aspire to achieve a quality of life for the community that meets, or even lifts, the aspi-rations of their neighbors and themselves. We greet today Evan Manning Frankel, Doctor of Letters, *honoris causa*.

It was an exquisite public acknowledgment of what those close to Evan had known for a long time. His friend Joseph Cullman said that even if Evan were not now working so dili-gently with the Jewish Center, he would have accomplished a great deal already. Surely the citation of the degree — "lifts the aspirations of neighbors and themselves" — precisely cap-tured Evan's achievement in perhaps its most poetic formula-tion.

XIII

Dr. Evan Frankel returned to pursue his goals at the Jewish Center with full vigor. When done with Evan's creative style, fund-raising raises not only money but also aspirations, responsibility, institutional program, and scope. When done properly, fund-raising stirs and renews an institution, for without growth and change, pruning here, expansion there, any organization will wilt and die. So Evan, in 1983, was helping to attract to the Jewish Center not only new money but also new blood. He was welcoming new people to participate in the life of the Jewish Center, just as he'd been attracting new people to live in East Hampton for nearly forty years. Among them was Peter Cohen, chief executive officer of Shearson/American Express, Inc., for whom the renowned residential architect Norman Jaffe had just completed a house on the South Fork. Not long afterward at the July 1983 annual congregational meeting, Evan was able to report that the hoped-for first-class new sanctuary now had an architect of the first order, for Norman Jaffe had volunteered his services and would be the architect for the Center's new building. Many architects are passionate about their work, and the architectural passions of Norman Jaffe were about to meet those of Evan Frankel with spectacular result for the Jewish Center.

As Evan continued to work toward the building campaign goal in the summer of 1983, he experienced a sad reminder of one reason why the Jewish Center had become so important to him: his brother Phil, in many ways Evan's early mentor and perhaps dearest to him of all the family, died at age ninety. Now only Mayer remained, and he was ailing. To the extent that the Center, and particularly the building of the new sanctuary, was, as Evan had often said, a gesture toward his family, it was now more important than ever to complete the task.

He raised money, he came to services regularly on Friday nights, and he spoke, hitting his themes often with the old-fashioned, orotund zeal of one who is proud to be a leader in the Jewish community. Dressed in his country squire tweeds or his cape, which by his own standards was very much "dressed up," Evan was not above admonishing congregants at times that, in his opinion, God did not approve of jeans and T-shirts at His sabbath services. Evan walked the Center grounds, plucking dandelions from the grass, and then he went inside to work with Betty Marmon and Rabbi Greenberg. On his way out he might stop to examine the pews to see how the wood was wearing. He was a hardworking, hands-on president as well as chief fund-raiser, and his aim throughout was that the Center be beautiful, proud, and exemplary of the best traditions of Jewish life. Nobody could say that Evan's attachment to the Center was "old-age" religion or fear-generated spirituality. Evan was not worried about his place in heaven, but rather about raising $1 million on earth. He was helping keep the Center together and on course out of a deep and enduring loyalty to the sources of his own being. This, according to Rabbi Greenberg, who worked closely with Evan, was the heart of Evan Frankel's piety. "Piety," said Greenberg, "was Aeneas carrying his father Anchises on his back out of burning Troy. It is Evan's carrying his past with him, through his leadership of the Jewish Center, into the future."

* * *

By the fireplace in the "ruin," the pool-to-be.

The McCord estate on Hither Lane at the time of purchase by
Evan, 1946. *Below:* Only months later, the former carriage
house refurbished.

The "ruin" being excavated, and, *below,* in use. "A pool is not a laundromat," Evan told his guests. "Off with your clothes!"

The pool, with landscaping complete.

Chou Chou Thors and Peggy Goldsmith seeing Evan off to
Italy for the filming of *The Medium*, 1950.

At the Forum in Rome.

A mock-heroic moment with Marie Powers, one of the stars of *The Medium.*

In London with *(left)* Sarah Churchill and *(far right)* Churchill's husband Anthony Beauchamp.

Arriving at the Sutton Place Theater with Sarah Churchill and Margaret Truman for the New York premiere of *The Medium*.

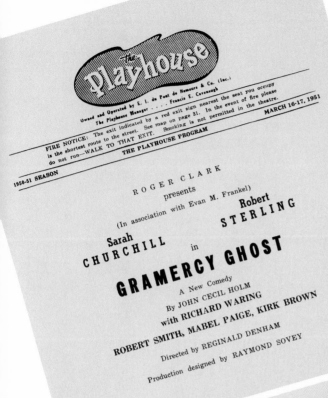

FIRE NOTICE: The exit indicated by a red exit sign nearest the seat you occupy is the shortest route to the street. See map on page 31. In the event of fire please do not run—WALK TO THAT EXIT. Smoking is not permitted in the theatre.

THE PLAYHOUSE PROGRAM

MARCH 16-17, 1951

Owned and Operated by E. I. du Pont de Nemours & Co. (Inc.)

The Playhouse Manager . . . . Francis E. Cavanaugh

1950-51 SEASON

ROGER CLARK

presents

(In association with Evan M. Frankel)

Sarah
CHURCHILL

Robert
STERLING

in

GRAMERCY GHOST

A New Comedy

By JOHN CECIL HOLM

with RICHARD WARING

ROBERT SMITH, MABEL PAIGE, KIRK BROWN

Directed by REGINALD DENHAM

Production designed by RAYMOND SOVEY

"GRAMERCY GHOST"

Playbill from Sarah Churchill's Broadway debut, in which she gave a "mettlesome" performance.

224

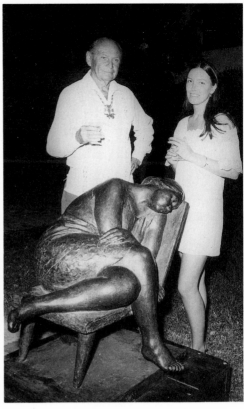

At the opening of a water desalinization plant in Israel, with
Senator Jacob Javits, 1963. *Right:* Before a Zuniga sculpture
with Elena Prohaska, Acapulco, 1968; *below,* at the Taj Mahal.

Vacationing in Jamaica with Margot and Leonard Gordon on
Evan's right, and Joan Cullman. *Below, left to right:* with Mr.
and Mrs. Ralph Lauren, Leigh Wells, and Raymond Bigar.

In the children's sculpture garden, Albert Price, Evan's gardener/sculptor, is seated beneath one of the figures he fashioned from discarded industrial metal. Flanking him are Evan and a houseboy. *Below:* Nora Bennett and the houseboy in the blooming garden.

Elena Prohaska
with a Raoul Hague
sculpture, at the
Upstairs Gallery,
East Hampton, 1972.

The collector beside
a familiar image.

Above, left: His two Straus godchildren, Tracy and Barney, Jr., 1967. *Left:* The godchildren grown up, and their mother, Joan Cullman.

Below left: Evan with Kari Lyn Jones and Andrew Sabin.

Below: Intoning the blessing over the bread at the *bar mitzvah* of Shawn Sabin, as the *bar mitzvah* boy looks on.

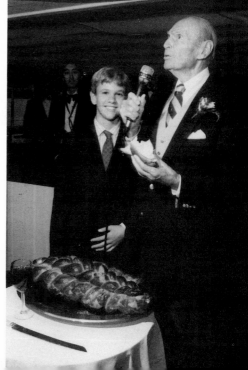

At the wedding of Joseph and Joan Cullman.

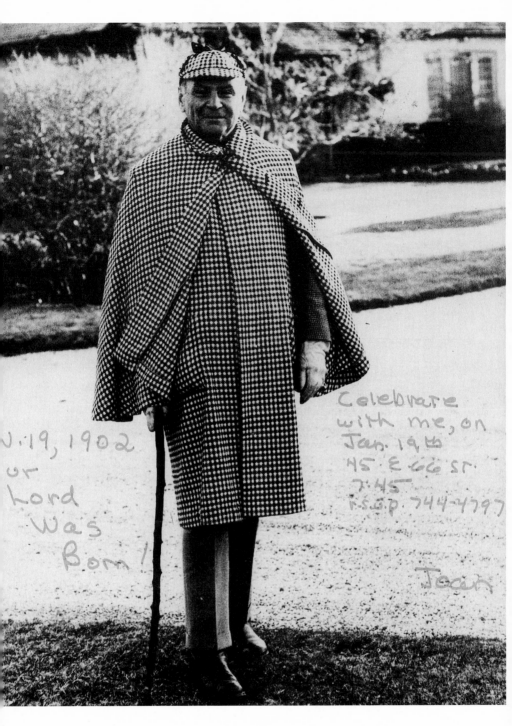

"Jan. 19, 1902, Our Lord was born!" Joan Cullman's invitation
to Evan's seventy-fifth birthday party.

One of Evan's "eloquent outrages." Protesting the introduction of convenience stores to East Hampton, 1983. *Below:* Beside his 1905 brougham, which he donated to the Amagansett Historical Society in 1984.

Evan's "girls" celebrating his eighty-fifth birthday. *(Back row, from left)*: Bobbi Weinstein, Magda Bleier, Patricia Heimann, Suzanne Pincus, Patrice Munsel; *(third row)* Susan Wood, Marilyn Salinger, Denise Regan, and the honored guest himself; *(second row)* Elena Prohaska Glinn, Joan Cullman, Elizabeth de Cuevas; *(front)* Leigh Wells, Jane Thors.

233

Kari Lyn Jones and Evan.

Burt Glinn,
Joe Cullman, Elena
Prohaska Glinn.

Elena, Evan, Andy Sabin.

Evan and the Cullmans.

234

Emerson Thors, Evan, Joe and Joan.

Joe, Evan's goddaughter Harrie Ellen Schloss, his nephews Ernest Frankel and David Plesser.

Flanked by nephews.

With Betty Marmon, as the scaffolding
of the Gates of the Grove sanctuary rises.

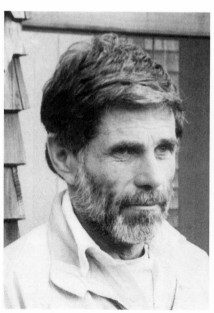

Photo: *The East Hampton Star*

Architect Norman Jaffe: "Evan
Frankel was the most difficult
client I have ever had, but the
result is the very best building
I have ever done."

With Attorney General Robert Abrams
at the fund-raising dedication of the
Gates of the Grove sanctuary, 1986.

In front of the copper beech on the grounds of the Jewish Center.

At the main entrance of the Jewish Center.

In the Memorial Grove.

At the entryway of the sanctuary, in a familiar pose to greet congregants.

Interior of the sanctuary of the Jewish Center before
installation of seats. Attorney General Abrams: "If you build a
synagogue, Maimonides advised centuries ago, it must be
more beautiful than your home. That's quite a mandate,
especially in the Hamptons! But here it's been done."

The exterior of the sanctuary, a marriage of the traditions of
East Hampton and the wooden synagogues of nineteenth-
century Poland, seen from Woods Lane.

At the *bemah,* the reader's platform: "And now our president, Evan Frankel, has a few words for us."

That future was again being threatened in East Hampton by development. But this time it was not the usual threat Evan and other long-time residents had fought before. It was no longer simply a battle against a particular subdivision, or a debate as to whether the local A & P should be allowed to build a tin, false mansard roof. No, what had been mounting for years, accelerated by the rolling wave of the whole Long Island land boom, now hit: a major reaction *against* the moderately successful controlled planning of the past decade on the South Fork.

By mid-summer of 1983, an alarming one hundred forty-five applications for residential subdivisions or new commercial construction had been filed in East Hampton, as compared with thirty-seven in all of 1982, and fifteen in 1981. Indeed, the current activity was described variously as a land rush and a fever, and Evan rightly predicted that the development in the five years to come would surpass all that had preceded. What he feared in 1972, when he'd been forced off the Village Planning Board, had come to pass by 1982. There was nearly a complete politicization of the town's central issue, planning and land-use policy. In February 1982, the Republican-controlled Town Board had abolished the Planning Department, which did research for the Planning Board. That sent a signal to developers, who pressed forward with their applications. In response, a grass-roots *ad hoc* organization, the Citizens Planning Committee, after a year's battle, forced the re-institution of the Planning Department. The gauntlet had been thrown down.

One Republican town official burst into tears at a meeting because she could not be heard above the billingsgate of her citizen opponents. Another asked his adversaries to roll up sleeves and step outside to finish their debate. On yet another occasion, there was a brouhaha when a town supervisor wore a gun to a Town Board session. He was only going to his gun club meeting afterwards, he told the local paper, but the Democrats would cause a stink about anything. Meanwhile, Evan and everyone else concerned with the integrity of East Hampton watched with alarm. They knew that the flood of applications for subdivision and new business development was motivated in part by the upcoming November election. If the Democrats swept in, builders feared even more stringent land preservation measures.

In September 1983, in the midst of his fund-raising campaign for the Jewish Center, Evan was also deciding what he could do about the dark clouds hovering over the land he cared so much about. Plans had been filed for the town's first shopping mall, and for its first "convenience" store. A tide of new motel applications had been submitted, several on the shores of unspoiled Three Mile Harbor. So despite the approaching High Holy Days — a particularly busy period for a temple president — Evan found the time and energy to do battle once more for the environment. Evan chose the Southland Corporation's proposed 7-Eleven store as the target of his fury.

Outrage, Evan had always maintained, could be a very useful tool. In fact, outrage had in many ways been Evan's stock-in-trade. It not only came to Evan the actor quite naturally, it was useful because it focused issues and galvanized people. The moment to employ it came on Friday night, September 22, 1983, in the East Hampton Town Hall. There hundreds of citizens were gathered to request a zoning change from the Town Board in order to prevent the 7-Eleven twenty-four-hour food store from opening on the Montauk Highway.

Prior to this hearing, Evan had worked with an *ad hoc* organization of nearby residents who had signed a petition to protest the store. Their representation at this meeting was to be the culmination of their efforts.

Further, Evan had a special concern in the matter, for the proposed convenience store would be practically in the front yard of his Sterns department store. Therefore, it was potentially threatening to one of his proudest and most significant achievements in East Hampton. What's more, Evan argued that the "retail strip" was the most damaging type of commercial development, the meanest cut of all, right through the skin of a town and bound for its heart. Although only one store — one zone — was in question this night, if the 7-Eleven could be defeated, a very important symbolic victory would be won, with immeasurable impact on the future.

Many people spoke emotionally, but Evan delivered the most impassioned plea. He warned that the 7-Eleven would be the opening wedge of an awful retail strip like North Highway in Southampton. "When I go through that highway," he said to the board and standing-room-only crowd, "and I remember what it was like, why it's a travesty!" He went on to admonish that, if allowed to happen, it would ultimately lead to juvenile vagrancy and drug problems. "I tell you, ladies and gentlemen," he declared, holding the microphone in a tightly clenched hand, "if that thing happens, I move out of here! And there are many here who will do the same. What do we want to do, destroy this lovely God-given place? Why, it's outrageous!" Evan relinquished the microphone and sat down, amid what *The East Hampton Star* described as thunderous applause.

The meeting, however, was far from over. There was a

caustic debate between the Town Board and Jack Campbell, who insisted on his right to sell his property to 7-Eleven. He called the requested zoning change confiscatory and accused the board, if it caved in to pressure, of being malicious and mendacious. "Who would want to buy a piece of property here," he asked, "when you could wake up the next morning and be in a different zone because you guys got together over a bottle of vodka?" Then he added, "This place is run like Guatemala!" When Campbell said that, in sum, he was being deprived of the rightful use of his land, Evan had had enough. He rose and engaged Campbell in a blistering shouting match, so the newspaper reported, "with the wealthy Hither Lane resident at one point offering 'to buy your goddamn property for what it was worth' to prevent the 7-Eleven from getting it." When Evan threatened to leave town, some people cried, "Go!" Others, responding to his vehement arguments, cheered him on.

Before the end of the meeting, Evan had one more scene to play. "I'm a bit of an actor," he said as he recalled that moment, "and I kept looking at the town supervisors, and holding up, so they could see it, a clipping I had with me and intended to read. You see, two days before the protest meeting I had read a revealing little article about these new neighbors we were going to have on Pantigo Road. So now I rose and got recognized and read the article. It seemed that the President and Vice-President of the Southland Corporation, the parent of 7-Eleven, were both under indictment for attempting to bribe the state tax official. That, I said, was what we were getting ready to bring into town!"

With that venality revealed, Evan had delivered the *coup de grace* to 7-Eleven. Lawsuits and counter-suits lingered on through the winter of 1984. Individuals continued to write to the paper that it *would* perhaps be good to have a place in town where one could get a quart of milk at midnight ("one 7-Eleven does not a Jericho Turnpike make"). However, the 7-Eleven store and what it represented had been resoundingly defeated. Six weeks later, in November, on a new wave of upzoning and slow-down-development initiatives, the Democrats swept into office.

XIV

In October 1983, Evan was back at work on the project that, he realized, mattered more to him than any other he had ever undertaken — the new building and sanctuary for the Jewish Center. It was going to be the most visible bearer of Evan's values, his taste, and his legacy in East Hampton, and it absolutely had to be right.

Although Evan had great confidence in the new architect — he had seen and liked the homes Norman Jaffe had built — he knew the task would not be easy. Perfection, which was nothing short of what he was now aspiring to, is never easy. Evan was not troubled by the fact that Jaffe had up to now built houses only for people, and not a single one for God. In many ways he saw this as a challenging plus, one that would help elicit from the architect the enthusiasm and inspiration that were the *sine qua non* for a perfect temple.

To make sure, however, that the project got off on the right foot, Evan sited the building himself, before Jaffe had put pen to paper to draw even a single line of the design. It was Evan, scrupulously protective of the trees and the landscape, who placed the new building on an east-west axis between the old building and the grove of giant arborvitae and spreading yews. At first Jaffe questioned Evan about his choice, but Evan had worked out precisely the new building's relationship to the Memorial Grove behind it, to the street, and the rest of the grounds. Although the architect quibbled, his client was steadfast. As it turned out, Evan's love of the trees and the landscape, which Jaffe likened to tree worship, would become one of the architect's own guiding inspirations for the building.

But in the fall of 1983, inspiration was still nine months, and several unacceptable design studies, away. Part of the problem was that, although there is a cubit-by-cubit Biblical blueprint for the temple in Jerusalem, visual architectural Jewish traditions are scant. While everyone agreed that a Solomonic edifice was definitely not the right model for East Hampton, what was? The only charge Evan had given to Jaffe as he began was the oxymoronic challenge: "Keep it simple *and* rich."

By winter 1983 Jaffe had submitted a plan. A committee of experienced New York City builders drawn from the membership was detailed to review the plans, but the committee was largely *pro forma*, and everything that went to the committee Jaffe had submitted to Evan first. Evan said nothing about this first plan. It generated little enthusiasm, languished, and became unacceptable. Jaffe submitted a second design study, and then, in the spring of 1984, a third. Each time Evan was, in Jaffe's phrase, "like a Jewish Mom," constantly questioning, challenging, withholding approval. "The first three plans were all interesting, warm, thoughtful," Jaffe recalled, "but the defect was that they were all expected. I began to understand then that Evan was looking for the unexpected, provided, of course, that it was also familiar!"

Jaffe toured American Jewish houses of worship, but found nothing in the pseudo-Moorish nineteenth-century temples or the glass and steel post-war suburban centers that seemed right for East Hampton, or for Evan Frankel.

The turning point came one evening in the summer of 1984 when Jaffe, Leonard Gordon, who was the Center's new vice-president, and Evan had dinner together. Evan told his architect the story of his sweatshop *bar mitzvah*. Jaffe, who also came from an orthodox, working-class Jewish background, said, "I saw in Evan then something I hadn't seen before. I saw beyond Evan the landholder and the man of the world, beyond the man of great charm and brilliant use of language. Beyond all that what I saw for the first time was the struggling Yiddish-speaking child lost in a Gentile world. This was true of me, too, of many of us. And I asked myself, Where did most of Evan's relatives, mine, and those of most of the Jews of East Hampton come from? The answer, of course, was Eastern Europe."

This insight sent Jaffe to the libraries in New York City, where he researched the architecture of Poland and Eastern Europe. But the critical source for him turned out to be much closer to home, a book of old photographs of nineteenth-century Polish synagogues that was in Rabbi Greenberg's own library. When Greenberg showed him these synagogues, built from about 1890 and all destroyed in the Holocaust, Jaffe knew he had hit pay dirt. For here were small shingled buildings set in rural, wooded landscapes not unreminiscent of the Memorial Grove.

"Here," said Jaffe, "I finally knew I had teachers. Here was a fresh, regional, informal, nonpretentious, but inspired group of buildings that fit unobtrusively into the *shtetls*. The lessons of the Polish synagogues were immediately apparent and applicable: The outside should disappear into the landscape, the building should be of homespun local materials, the inside should ascend, surprisingly, to unanticipated heights, and everything should be enhanced by detail and craftsmanship unexpected from the humble outside."

Not until he studied this architecture had Jaffe realized

that it was going to be possible to fulfill Evan's mandate, to keep the temple simple and simultaneously rich, unexpected and yet familiar. For what possibly could be more surprisingly familiar to Evan Frankel of Bukochevich and East Hampton than a new temple on Woods Lane inspired by the architecture of his native Cracow region? As he pored over the photographs, a quotation from the Talmud floated back to Jaffe in memory: "Poverty adorns the Jew as a red ribbon a white horse." With that, Jaffe really knew he had it: "I realized that it was not what the building is," he said, "but what it is *not* that will count. Therefore, for my fourth attempt, I sought grace and even power in restraint, humility, and simplicity."

He decided, however, not to tell Evan — not yet. He set to work enthusiastically, even obsessively. Within two months he was ready. One night in late summer he showed slides to Evan and Leonard Gordon. Jaffe will not soon forget that night: "Evan lay in his bed nursing a small cold, and I showed the slides to him there, right in the bedroom. Leonard was enthusiastic. But Evan said nothing, absolutely nothing, at first. After a while, he turned to me and said, 'Do you really think you have it?'

"*I* knew I had it, and I'm convinced Evan knew too, but like a Yiddish skeptic, he was continually asking me, 'Do you have it?' I think he was deliberately restraining enthusiasm, as any task master does, knowing that my craving for his enthusiasm would somehow release me from the responsibility of testing my own work and going deeper. And he knew it! He literally never showed any enthusiasm until the building was done, and while from this point on he left the work for me to do totally on my own at every stage, he was always there asking the questions of the classic Jewish teacher, like a never-ending refrain: 'Do you have it? Are you certain you have it?'

"I tell you," Jaffe said, with the relief of hindsight, "it was the way a pianist learns to do a thing because the parent holds back, driving you to endless practice, and the reward only comes when the concert is played!"

Evan could now announce matter-of-factly, in his fall 1984 message to congregants, that design plans were finally complete and the architect was proceeding with structural and mechanical drawings. The hope was for construction to commence in the early spring of 1985.

If Evan's controlled and questioning tone with the architect concealed a secret and growing elation, that mood was deeply affected in June 1984, by news that Karole Spector had died. She had been a member of the Center's board of trustees, founder and director of the Jewish Center's very successful summer camp, and a close and indefatigable colleague of Evan's in the growth of the Center. It was a great loss, lightened only a little by the leap in membership at the temple she cared so much about. Between the High Holidays and year-end 1984, sixty new members had joined, bringing the roster of the congregation to nearly three hundred families by February 1985. These new families did not just join and disappear, because Evan made it his business to welcome personally and publicly each new family; in effect he initiated them into membership by calling them to the *bemah* during Friday night services and presenting them with engraved certificates. Some people, Evan said, enjoyed receiving these as if they had just been made Doctors of Humanities! Anticipation of the groundbreaking in the spring was infectious.

But when late spring arrived, not enough money had. Although he was terribly saddened, in April, by the death at age

251

ninety-five of his last remaining sibling, his brother Mayer, Evan had to redouble his efforts. "I have striven," he wrote to the congregants, like a character out of Dickens or Conan Doyle, "with might and main to make our fund-raising a completely voluntary action on your part, and I know you will vindicate my approach with your generosity!"

And they did. In the summer of 1985, without ceremony or fanfare, as if that would delay the completion of the task, ground was broken, excavation begun, and a 5,200-square-foot foundation was poured. Evan had raised $750,000 of the $1.3 million estimated to be required for completion of the building. Now, therefore, was not the moment to rest, and Evan continued his fund-raising and promotion of the Jewish Center at his usual electric pace. Right before the High Holidays, Evan received a call from his friend Michael Bassett, owner of Bassett House Inn, East Hampton. As he had many times with many others, Evan had lent an important hand when Bassett started his business. Bassett had guests that fall weekend who wanted to go to High Holiday services, and he, the good host, had called Evan to inquire. "Evan began to talk," Bassett remembered, "and tell me all about the Jewish Center and its fund-raising campaign and his goal, and he said he'd throw in two High Holiday tickets if *I* joined the temple as a member for $600. 'Evan,' I told him, 'Whoa! Slow down. I just want two tickets for services this one weekend. They're not for me. They're for my guests. I'm not even Jewish.' But Evan, unperturbed, went on with his pitch."

After services that year, beneath a tent that had grown still larger to accommodate the crowd, contributions and letters of praise and encouragement filled the mailbox at Hither Lane. These fueled Evan's resolve to maintain the momentum of the fund-raising campaign. The building's architect took the unusual step of personally raising $15,000 for the project. This strenuous effort, Jaffe reported, enormously increased his awe of Evan's fund-raising prowess. By winter, when many congregants were going off for their vacations and their longest hiatus away from East Hampton, the steel frame of the sanctuary had been raised, and, along with it, sufficient funds for Jaffe to begin focusing on the interior.

When Evan returned to East Hampton in March 1986 and visited the new sanctuary-in-the-making, he found that rain and cold had prevented much additional work from being done. However, this most unusual of temple presidents was moved to paraphrase for the membership, in his first message of 1986, lines from the opera *Tannhaüser:* "Once more, dear Center, I with rapture behold thee and greet the fields that so sweetly enfold thee."

Evan's rapture, however, was primarily for fund-raising purposes and presidential messages. He wasn't letting his architect see much of it. In fact, the more the building began to come to life, the more Evan's tension increased, for the building at all costs had to be right. There was, however, one moment in the spring of 1986 when his anxiety slipped out. Jaffe remembered the scene: "We were alone, Evan and I, in the shell of the building. The portico in front of the ark had just been framed in, and Evan walked away from me and stood in front of it, alone. Then he spread his arms, clenched his fists, and shook them at the sky, repeating, 'Must it be like this? Must it be like this?'"

Evan said nothing else. His exclamation was not, apparently, meant as a criticism of Jaffe's work, and the two men stood in silence. Whatever Evan meant, riveted there, his legs and arms spread like an Old Testament patriarch, priest, or prophet at the future entry to the ark of the Lord, he kept to himself.

Evan, however, experienced a difficult time during the next month or two. He had a cataract operation, which went well, and he was, in Rabbi Greenberg's phrase, "back in the temple and reading the small Hebrew print in the prayer book" within two weeks. Soon afterward, however, Evan was in a traffic accident. He escaped serious injury but had lacerations and abrasions on his arms and face. Although he carried himself erect as ever, there was something about the accident that, in the estimate of his closest friends, had shaken Evan up in a way the accumulation of his eighty-four busy years had not.

All the more reason to get on with the work. By June, the exterior of the sanctuary building was nearly complete. Built of East Hampton's original materials, cedar shakes, and flowing naturally out from the adjacent Victorian Borden house, the new sanctuary so far had achieved its aim by effectively echoing the lost wooden synagogues of Poland. It was as if one had magically been saved from the fires of Europe to reappear a half century later on the South Fork. The building, through careful exterior detailing, also mediated between the new and the old, between Jewish traditions and those of East Hampton. Jaffe had placed on the walls at eye level a band of simple decorative shingles, in the form of stars of David. Such shingle work not only was common in local Victorian houses, but would have been a concept understood by the synagogue builders of Eastern Europe as well. With the windows looking out onto the Memorial Grove, and the roof glass letting the northern light fill the ascending interior portico spaces, it was evident already that Evan's siting worked perfectly. Clearly Jaffe, for whom this job was now nearly as much of a mission as it was for Evan, had delivered the soaring, spiritual interior he had promised.

The building was unfinished and unfurnished, and a great deal remained to be done, but so far, so good. A dedicatory celebration was definitely in order. Furthermore, Evan needed the occasion to raise more money to complete the sanctuary. The date chosen was August 31, 1986.

Over four hundred people came to the sanctuary-under-construction and to the Memorial Grove that day. It was a major event, not only to mark the building's "birth" in East Hampton but to recognize the man whose dream it had been. Because Evan's energy had an ageless quality, it was easy to forget that he was soon to be eighty-five years old. The main speaker was Attorney General of New York Robert Abrams, who was rushed to the scene by State Troopers when his car broke down forty miles west of East Hampton. Five years before, Abrams and Evan had presided at a symbolic ground-breaking for a soon-to-be abandoned addition to the Center. Now he was pleased to be present to dedicate the structure that had finally evolved.

"The point of Evan's dream and vision," the Attorney General said, "was to build a Jewish house of worship to encourage people to come together. Centuries ago Maimonides advised," he went on, "that if you build a synagogue, it must be more beautiful than your home. That's quite a mandate, especially in the Hamptons! But here it's been done."

Among the many guests were the mayor of East Hampton, the Reverend Frederick Schultz of the First Presbyterian Church, and East Hampton Town Supervisor Judith Hope.

255

Hope wrote about Evan shortly afterward in her column in the *Star*: "Mr. Frankel's vision and leadership have influenced many aspects of our community over the years. A major landowner, he set very high standards of responsibility and stewardship toward the environment. By his personal example he proved that sensitive development, development that respected the delicate integrity of nature, was viable.

"All of us in East Hampton owe Evan Frankel a debt of gratitude for his leadership. I am especially happy that his dearly held dream of the new sanctuary has at long last become a reality."

The rising crescendo of praise for the new sanctuary, from both the Jewish and non-Jewish communities, was Evan's real eighty-fifth birthday present.

There was another eighty-fifth birthday celebration for Evan, both more frivolous and, in some ways, more poignant. It took place in December, when the women in Evan's life decided to throw a party for him with the theme "Evan's Girls." All men, except of course the honored guest, were excluded. Gathered around him at the home of Suzanne Pincus in Manhattan were the women Evan adored: friends and girlfriends, pals, "daughters," confidants, lovers, and everyone in between. Perhaps none knew Evan better than these women or came closer to understanding the mystery who was Evan Frankel. They knew that he was both very Jewish and had also been drawn to non-Jewish worlds; that he was both gregarious and in need of solitude; that he was simultaneously tough and vulnerable; that he had a high libidinal charge and love of women but had decided early in life not to marry; that he had pursued success and glamour vigorously, but with the full knowledge that true values lay in family love and community.

Joan Cullman might have asked then at the party, as she did often: "Will the real Evan Frankel please stand up?" The answer, of course, was that here was a man who was not only the product of a grand and fast-disappearing age, but also one who had, to a great extent, truly invented himself. If he was a mystery, it was only that Evan Frankel was — is — a man perfectly, gracefully balanced in his contradictions, like a high-wire artist of life.

Only Amy Small and Harrie Ellen Schloss could not join in the merrymaking for Evan's eighty-fifth with Bobbie Weinstein, Magda Bleier, Patricia Heimann, Patrice Munsel, Susan Wood, Leigh Wells, Jane Thors, Marilyn Salinger, Denise Regan, Elena Prohaska Glinn, Peggy Goldsmith, Joan Cullman, and Elizabeth de Cuevas. The walls were festooned with photographs documenting — as Emerson Thors might have said — the honored guest's lifetime of utter indifference to the pursuit of the Female. Suzanne Pincus and Joan Cullman delivered a poem for Evan, Leigh Wells read aloud the "diploma" she had fashioned for him. Every one of Evan's girls, in fact, offered a tribute or testimonial. If one calculated from the allotted lifespan of three score and ten, this eighty-fifth birthday soirée was like a hilarious sweet sixteen party of Evan's second lifetime.

XV

In the spring of 1987, Betty Marmon, the secretary of the Center's board, noticed that Evan's routine tongue-in-cheek complaints about his administrative duties at the Center seemed to have grown a little more serious. "I'm tired," he said to her one day. "Why don't you and I leave all this behind and go back to Jamaica?"

"All right," Betty answered — one had to have a sense of humor to work closely with Evan — "but I'll only run off with you if you absolutely promise to remain as president. We need you!"

In June of 1987, however, a month before the annual membership meeting, and ten years after he'd assumed the job of president, Evan resigned. Although he had already garnered over $1 million for the Center since 1982, he was by no means through with fund-raising. Since the building was a reality, with largely only the interior remaining to be finished, it seemed prudent for Evan to relinquish his administrative chores. Leonard Gordon was elected the new president on July 26, 1987. Evan was named chairman of the board, and from this new desk he sallied forth toward his eighty-sixth birthday as passionate as ever about the sanctuary and community-building he had undertaken.

The ceremony of the preceding August at the construction site had been a dedication but not a debut for the sanctuary. With the High Holidays approaching, there was much still unfinished in the interior, and many key decisions for Norman

Jaffe and Evan to make. Although the upcoming holidays would, as usual, be held in the adjacent tent, the new sanctuary would be experienced *in toto* by the congregants for the very first time when it was used for Evan's traditional Memorial Grove ceremony.

Evan's concern for the perfection of the new sanctuary space accelerated, but he tried not to show his anxiety to Jaffe. In the summer of 1987, Evan traveled very little. Nearly every day he visited the stonemasons and the carpenters at work on the interior. The masons were setting the floor stones in a deliberately random pattern to echo the limestone walls of Jerusalem. The carpenters were working at a frenetic pace affixing to the walls and the supporting columns of the porticoes the silky smooth boards of Alaska yellow cedar. Jaffe had chosen this wood for the sanctuary precisely because no residence in town was likely to have it. It was both rich and simple, just as Evan had required it. Incised in these interior walls, at the tops of the columns, in the paneling of the roof, in the handrails, in the *bemah*, and in the window frames, even in the interior of the otherwise unadorned ark, was the motif of rising and angling lines, a tree symbol — Evan's beloved trees — with trunk and arms branching out. Where the ascending vertical lines met the horizontals at the ceiling and skylights, an architectural canopy of wood, line, and light was created, as if Evan, working through Jaffe, had finally been able to bring outside inside.

As the craftsmen worked to get the sanctuary as near to completion as possible for the 1987 High Holiday observance, Evan did not just encourage them in their work but, in Jaffe's word, *bonded* himself to them. Evan wanted the workers to know they were not building anonymously, but for a person, for Evan Frankel.

Moreover, Evan loved what he saw. What he conveyed effortlessly — because it came naturally to him — was a love and appreciation for all the craftsmanship and detail. Evan beheld the sanctuary as it came to life through the eyes of the early twentieth-century builder that he had been and was, a man who had run a construction firm in America when craftsmanship was still familiar and highly valued. "The key to the entire building," Jaffe said recently, "was that Evan understood and appreciated craftsmanship, the power of simple materials elevated by the touch of the human hand."

As Evan returned again and again, he saw the ten sections surrounding the main sanctuary space gradually being framed in. The sections, each named for one of the ten cabalistic virtues, the *sefirot* in Hebrew, were like symbolic mystical tree branches ascending, five on each side, toward the ark at the top. The ark itself was recessed dramatically and framed by the trees of the Memorial Grove outside. Evan told Jaffe that it was particularly important that the *bemah* be inspiring, substantial, and durable, and so the decision was made to build it and the pews of white ash. Evan continued to appreciate what he saw, and he persevered in raising funds so the job might be completed and perfection attained. The amount required, now nearing $2 million, was reachable because Evan decided he was going to reach it. The sanctuary was now more than ever, for both architect and founder, a labor of love.

Although the weather was not obliging, over a thousand worshippers came to the tent for services on September 24. Nearby, the new sanctuary, officially named the Gates of the Grove, was without pews, and the basement, reception, and classroom space were still unfinished, but it was otherwise complete, serene, and beautiful. The worshippers could see that the man who for the past ten years had virtually personified the Jewish Center of the Hamptons had, with his architect, delivered a building that was as unique and distinctive as Evan Frankel.

As was his custom, Evan clasped hands with as many of the worshippers as possible, but this Rosh Hashana, the salutations were not only "Good Yontif," and "Happy New Year," but also "Mazel Tov" on the near completion of his ten-year labor. The congratulations conveyed to him would soon be reflected in the architectural awards and the press reviews that cited the building not only as "a significant contribution to devotional architecture," but also one that clearly "deserved an exceptional place among post-war synagogues in this country and Europe." Evan, of course, had been building not only a temple, but, through it, a community that would be exemplary and long-lived, and it was the material evidence of that — the large congregation crowding around him — that gave him the greatest satisfaction.

During a break in the services, Evan finally showed his pride and appreciation to Jaffe and said to his architect, "Norman, you may have been the mother of this all, but I was the father."

Norman Jaffe said later, "Evan Frankel was the most difficult client I have ever had, but the result is the very best building I have ever done."

Ten days later, on October 4, 1987, as a rainy, cold, and dank Yom Kippur ended, Evan stepped out of the tent, his duties completed for one more year. He was thinking that the place still needed work, and he certainly planned to consider carefully every single new tree and plant, type and size, that was proposed for the beloved grounds around the new sanctuary. Then, suddenly, amazingly for Evan, because nothing like this had ever happened before, his legs felt as if they might go out from under him. Like a marathon runner with his goal finally in sight, Evan nearly collapsed, in view of the new sanctuary. A friend drove him home. That night, Evan found himself suddenly shivering. Later, in his bedroom, he fell to the floor. He did not know, as he lost consciousness, that he was about to take on another challenge. This one he did not want. It was to be the long winter's fight for his life.

EPILOGUE

Rosh Hashana, 5748/September 12, 1988

Beneath the white tent of the Jewish Center of the Hamptons, Evan Frankel rose to speak. He was dressed in a white suit and white skullcap and wrapped in a white prayer shawl. His face and eyes were very clear.

"Dear friends, ladies and gentlemen," he began, "I had a dream recently. In it I was called to speak to God, and I spent two days up there with him, and frankly I thought I had had it, that my life was done. But then God said to me, 'Evan, you are not going to die. I know the doctors said you were, but what do doctors know? You are going to live because you have some more work to do. You built me a house, but your mission's not through yet. Go back to that house you built me, and endow it. Make sure it is used right, to teach Hebrew and the values of my prophets, and to build community.'

"So I obviously couldn't die yet, ladies and gentlemen, and here I am!"

Evan went on, to hit his themes once again, and when he was done, the thousand worshippers broke out in wave upon wave of warm, tumultuous applause. They were not supposed to do that, on the High Holidays in a house of prayer. Indeed nothing like this had ever happened before. But it was Evan Frankel, founder of the Gates of the Grove sanctuary of the Jewish Center, and Squire of East Hampton, for whom they were applauding, and in that case, God could wink and look the other way.

BIBLIOGRAPHY

Epstein, Jason, and Elizabeth Barlow. *East Hampton, A History and Guide*. New York: Random House, 1985

Gorelick, Sherry. *City College and the Jewish Poor*. New York: Schocken Books, 1982

Hapgood, Hutchins. *The Spirit of the Ghetto*, ed. Moses Rischin. Cambridge, Mass.: Belknap Press of Harvard University, 1967

Howe, Irving, and Kenneth Libo. *How We Lived, A Documentary History of Immigrant Jews in America 1880-1930*. New York: Richard Marek, 1979

Kessner, Thomas. *The Golden Door*. New York: Oxford University Press, 1977

Rattray, Everett T. *The South Fork, The Land and the People of Eastern Long Island*. New York: Random House, 1979

Rosolenko, Harry. *The Time That Was*. New York: The Dial Press, 1971

Sanders, Ronald. *The Lower East Side, A Guide To Its Jewish Past in 99 Photographs*. New York: Dover Publications, 1979

Wurts, Richard. *The New York World's Fair 1939/1940 in 155 Pictures*. New York: Dover Publications, 1977

About the Author

Allan Appel has published two books of poetry and four novels, most recently *The Rabbi of Casino Boulevard* (New York: St. Martin's Press, 1986). This is his first biography. He lives in New York City with his wife and two children.

This book was produced for the publisher,
by Ray Freiman & Company
Stamford, Connecticut 06903